**Praise for *The Body Is Not an Apology***

P9-CKT-405

"From the moment I met Sonya Renee, I knew my life, my world, and the way I view myself and others around me would never be the same. *The Body Is Not an Apology* is essential reading for those of us who crave understanding and those who are already on the path to learning how beautiful and complex our bodies are. It will empower you with the tools to navigate a world that is often unkind to those of us who whether by choice or design don't adhere to society's standard of beauty. Her words will echo in your heart, soul, and body just as they have in mine."

—**Tess Holliday, plus model, author, and founder of Eff Your Beauty Standards**

"*The Body Is Not an Apology* is a gift, a blessing, a prayer, a reminder, a sacred text. In it, Taylor invites us to live in a world where different bodies are seen, affirmed, celebrated, and just. Taylor invites us to break up with shame, to deepen our literacy, and to liberate our practice of celebrating every body and never apologizing for this body that is mine and takes care of me so well. This book cracked me open in ways that I'm so grateful for. I know it will do the same for you."

—**Alicia Garza, cocreator of the Black Lives Matter Global Network and Strategy + Partnerships Director, National Domestic Workers Alliance**

"*The Body Is Not an Apology* is a radical, merciful, transformational book that will give you deep insights, inspiration, and concrete tools for launching the revolution right inside your own beloved body. Written from deep experience, with a force of catalytic energy and so much love."

—**Eve Ensler, author of *The Vagina Monologues* and *In the Body of the World***

"In 2017, #thefirsttimeisawmyself was a trending hashtag and Netflix campaign. As a disabled woman, #thefirsttimeireadmyself may well have been this book. Thank you, Sonya. Bought two copies, one for me and one for my daughter."

—**Rebecca Cokely, Senior Fellow for Disability Policy, Center for American Progress, disability rights activist, and mom**

"Sonya Renee Taylor is a treasure that this world simply does not deserve. *The Body Is Not an Apology* is the gift of radical love the world needs! We are all better off because of her presence, talent, compassion, and authentic work. Thank you, Sonya, for all that you do."

—**Jes Baker, aka The Militant Baker, author of *Things No One Will Tell Fat Girls***

"In these times, when the search for answers to the mounting injustices in our world seems to confound us, Sonya Renee Taylor offers a simple but powerful place to begin: recovering our relationship with our own bodies. To build a world that works for everyone, we must first make the radical decision to love every facet of ourselves. Through lucid and courageous self-revelation, Taylor shows us how to realize the revolutionary potential of self-love. 'The body is not an apology' is the mantra we should all embrace."

—**Kimberlé Crenshaw, legal scholar and founder and Executive Director, African American Policy Forum**

# The Body Is Not an Apology

# The Body Is Not an Apology

## *The Power of Radical Self-Love*

## Sonya Renee Taylor

Berrett–Koehler Publishers, Inc.
*a BK Life book*

**Berrett-Koehler Publishers, Inc.**
1333 Broadway, Suite 1000
Oakland, CA 94612-1921
Tel: (510) 817-2277   Fax: (510) 817-2278   www.bkconnection.com

**Ordering Information**
**Quantity sales.** Special discounts are available on quantity purchases by corporations, associations, and others. For details, contact the "Special Sales Department" at the Berrett-Koehler address above.
**Individual sales.** Berrett-Koehler publications are available through most bookstores. They can also be ordered directly from Berrett-Koehler: Tel: (800) 929-2929; Fax: (802) 864-7626; www.bkconnection.com.
**Orders for college textbook/course adoption use.** Please contact Berrett-Koehler: Tel: (800) 929-2929; Fax: (802) 864-7626.

Distributed to the U.S. trade and internationally by Penguin Random House Publisher Services.

Berrett-Koehler and the BK logo are registered trademarks of Berrett-Koehler Publishers, Inc.

Printed in the United States of America

Berrett-Koehler books are printed on long-lasting acid-free paper. When it is available, we choose paper that has been manufactured by environmentally responsible processes. These may include using trees grown in sustainable forests, incorporating recycled paper, minimizing chlorine in bleaching, or recycling the energy produced at the paper mill.

**Library of Congress Cataloging-in-Publication Data**

Name: Taylor, Sonya Renee, author.
Title: The body is not an apology : the power of radical self-love / Sonya Renee Taylor.
Description: Oakland, CA : Berrett-Koehler Publishers, [2018] | Includes bibliographical references and index.
Identifiers: LCCN 2017028473 | ISBN 9781626569768 (pbk.)
Subjects: LCSH: Self-acceptance. | Self-perception. | Body image. | Human body.
Classification: LCC BF575.S37 T39 2018 | DDC 158.1—dc23
LC record available at https://lccn.loc.gov/2017028473.

First Edition
25  24  23  22  21  20  19        15  14  13  12  11  10  9  8

Set in Arno Pro by Westchester Publishing Services
Interior design by Laurel Muller
Cover design by Irene Morris, Morris Design
Cover Image by Carey Lynne Fruth from the viral photo series "American Beauty"

**For Terry Lyn Hines (1959–2012)**
My first and most enduring example
of the power of radical love.

### My Mother's Belly

*The bread of her waist, a loaf*
*I would knead with eight-year-old palms*
*sweaty from play. My brother and I marveled*
*at the ridges and grooves. How they would summit at her navel.*
*How her belly looked like a walnut. How we were once seeds*
*that resided inside. We giggled, my brother and I,*
*when she would recline on the couch,*
*lift her shirt, let her belly spread like cake batter in a pan.*
*It was as much a treat as licking the sweet from electric mixers on birthdays.*

*The undulating of my mother's belly was not*
*a shame she hid from her children.*
*She knew we came from this. Her belly was a gift*
*we kept passing between us.*
*It was both hers, of her body,*
*and ours for having made it new,*
*different. Her belly was an altar of flesh*
*built in remembrance of us, by us.*

*What remains of my mother's belly*
*resides in a container of ashes I keep in a closet.*
*Every once and again, I open the box,*
*sift through the fine crystals with palms*
*that were once eight. Feel the grooves and ridges*
*that do not summit now but rill through fingers.*
*Granules so much more salt*
*than sweet today. And yet, still I marvel*
*at her once body. Even in this form say,*
*"I came from this."*

# Contents

# Prologue

Long before there was a digital media and education company or a radical self-love movement with hundreds of thousands of followers on our website and social media pages, before anyone cared to write about us in newsprint or interview me on television, before people began to send me photos of their bodies with my words etched in ink on their backs, forearms, and shoulders (which never stops being awesome and weird), there was a word . . . well, words. Those words were "your body is not an apology." It was the summer of 2010, in a hotel room in Knoxville, Tennessee. My team and I were preparing for evening bouts in competition at the Southern Fried Poetry Slam. Slam is competitive performance poetry. Teams and individuals get three minutes onstage to share what is often deeply intimate, personal, and political poetry, at which point five randomly selected judges from the audience score their poems on a scale from 0.0 to 10.0. It's a raucous game that takes the high art of poetry and brings it to the masses in bars, clubs, coffee shops, and National Poetry Slam Championship Tournaments around the country. Poetry slam is as ridiculous as it is beautiful; it is everything gauche and glorious about the power of the word. The slam is a place where the misfit and the marginalized (and the self-absorbed) have center stage and the rapt ears of an audience, if only for three minutes.

It was on a hotel bed in this city, preparing for this odd game, that I uttered the words "your body is not an apology" for the first time. My team was a kaleidoscope of bodies and identities. We were a microcosm of a world I would like to live in. We were Black, White, Southeast Asian. We are able bodied and disabled. We were gay, straight, bi, and queer. What we brought to Knoxville that year were the stories of living in our bodies in all their complex tapestries. We were complicated and honest with each other, and this is how I wound up in a conversation with my teammate Natasha, an early-thirtysomething living with cerebral palsy and fearful she might be pregnant. Natasha told me how her potential pregnancy was most assuredly by a guy who was just an occasional fling. All of life was up in the air for Natasha, but she was abundantly clear that she had no desire to have a baby and not by this person. One of my many career iterations of the past was as a sexual-health and public-health service provider. This background made me notorious for asking people about their safer-sex practices, handing out condoms, and offering sexual-health harm-reduction strategies. Instinctually, I asked Natasha why she had chosen not to use a condom with this casual sexual partner with whom she had no interest in procreating. Neither Natasha nor I knew that my honest question and her honest answer would be the catalyst for a movement. Natasha told me her truth: "My disability makes sex hard already, with positioning and stuff. I just didn't feel like it was okay to make a big deal about using condoms."

When we hear someone's truth and it strikes some deep part of our humanity, our own hidden shames, it can be easy to recoil into silence. We struggle to hold the truths of others because we have so rarely had the experience of having our own truths held. Social researcher and expert on vulnerability and shame Brené Brown says, "If we can share our story with someone who responds with empathy and understanding, shame can't survive."[1] I understood the truth Natasha was sharing. Her words pricked some painful underbelly of knowing in my own body. My entire being rang in resonance. I was transported to all the times I had given away my own body in penance. A reel of memories scrolled through my mind of all the ways I told the world I was sorry for having this wrong, bad body. It was from this deep cave of mutual vulnerability that the words spilled from me, "Natasha, your body is not an apology. It is not something you give to someone to say, 'Sorry for my disability.'" She began to weep, and for a few minutes I just held my maybe-pregnant friend as she contemplated the fullness of what those words meant for her life and her body. There are times when our unflinching honesty, vulnerability, and empathy will create a transformative portal, an opening to a completely new way of living. Such a portal was created between Natasha and me that summer evening in Tennessee, because as the words escaped my lips some part of them remained stuck inside me. The words I said to Natasha in that hotel room were as much for me as they were for her. I was also telling myself, "Sonya, your body is not an apology."

At every turn, for days after my conversation with Natasha, the words returned to me like some sort of cosmic boomerang. They kept echoing off the walls of all my hidden hurts. Every time I uttered a disparaging word about my dimpled thighs I'd hear, "Your body is not an apology, Sonya." Each time I marked some erroneous statement with "My bad. I'm so stupid," my own inner voice would retort, "Your body is not an apology." Whenever my critical eye focused laser-like on some perceived imperfection of my own or some other human's being, the words would arrive like a well-trained butler to remind me, "Hey, the body is not an apology." My poet self knew that the words were demanding to be more than a passing conversation with a friend. They wanted more than my own self-flagellation. The words always had their own plans. Me, I was just a vessel.

I recently listened to famed author and spiritual teacher Marianne Williamson share a talk on relationships. In it, she described the principle of natural intelligence. She posited, "An acorn does not have to say, 'I intend to become an oak tree.' Natural intelligence intends that every living thing become the highest form of itself and designs us accordingly."[2] In a single sentence, all in me that felt nameless was named. We have a dictionary full of terms describing our interpretation of natural intelligence. We sometimes call it purpose; other times, destiny. Although I agree with the spirit of those terms, I believe they fail to encapsulate the fullness of what Marianne Williamson's acorn example illustrates. Both *purpose* and *destiny* allude to a place we might, with enough effort, someday arrive. We belabor ourselves with all the things we must do to fulfill our purpose or live out our destiny. Contrary to purpose, natural intelligence does not require we do anything to achieve it. Natural intelligence imbues us with all we need at this exact moment to manifest the highest form of ourselves, and we don't have to figure out how to get it. We arrived on this planet with this source material already present. I am by no means implying that the work you may have done up to this point has been useless. To the contrary, I applaud whatever labor you have undertaken that has gotten you this far. Survival is damn hard. Each of us has traversed a gauntlet of traumas, shames, and fears to be where we are today, wherever that is. Each day we wake to a planet full of social, political, and economic obstructions that siphon our energy and diminish our sense of self. Consequently, tapping into this natural intelligence often feels nearly impossible. Humans unfortunately make being human exceptionally hard for each other, but I assure you, the work we have done or will do is not about acquiring some way of being that we currently lack. The work is to crumble the barriers of injustice and shame leveled against us so that we might access what we have always been, because we will, if unobstructed, inevitably grow into the purpose for which we were created: our own unique version of that oak tree.

I have my own name for natural intelligence. I call it radical self-love. Radical self-love was the force that cannoned the words "your body is not an apology" out of my mouth, directed toward a friend but ultimately barreling into my own chest and then into the hearts of hundreds of thousands of people around the world. Evangelizing radical self-love as the transformative foundation of how we make peace with our bodies, make peace with the bodies of others, and ultimately change the world is my highest calling. Coincidence after seeming coincidence has made that much evident. I don't know what your highest calling is. It's possible you don't quite know either. That is perfect. At this very second, a trembling acorn is plummeting from a branch, clueless as to why. It doesn't need to know why to fulfill its calling; it just needs us to get out of its way. Radical self-love is an engine inside you driving you to make your calling manifest. It is the exhaustion you feel every time the whispers of self-loathing, body shame, and doubt skulk through your brain. It is the contrary impulse that made you open this book, an action driven by a force so much larger than the voice of doubt and yet sometimes so much more difficult to hear.

Radical self-love is not a destination you are trying to get to; it is who you already are, and it is already working tirelessly to guide your life. The question is how can you listen to it more distinctly, more often? Even over the blaring of constant body shame? How can you allow it to change your relationship with your body and your world? And how can that change ripple throughout the entire planet? At the organization I founded, The Body Is Not an Apology, we are not saying anything new (see www.TheBodyIsNotAnApology.com). We are, however, connecting some straggling dots we believe others may have missed along the way. We know that the answer has always been love. The question is how do we stop forgetting the answer so we can get on with living our highest, most radically unapologetic lives. This book is my most sincere effort to help us all answer that.

# The Body Is Not an Apology

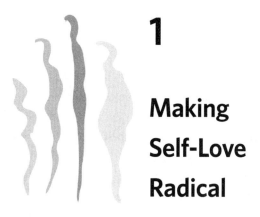

# 1

# Making Self-Love Radical

## What Radical Self-Love Is and What It Ain't

Let me answer a couple of questions right away before you dig too deeply into this book and are left feeling bamboozled and hoodwinked. First, "Will this book fix my self-esteem, Sonya?" Nope. Second, "Will this book teach me how to have self-confidence?" Nah. Impromptu third question, "Well then why in Hades am I reading this book?" You are reading this book because your heart is calling you toward something exponentially more magnanimous and more succulent than self-esteem or self-confidence. You are being called toward radical self-love. While not completely unrelated to self-esteem or self-confidence, radical self-love is its own entity, a lush and verdant island offering safe harbor for self-esteem and self-confidence. Unfortunately, those two ships often choose to wander aimlessly adrift at sea, relying on willpower or ego to drive them, and in the absence of those motors are left hopelessly pursuing the fraught mirage of someday. As in, "Someday I will feel good enough about myself to shop that screenplay I wrote." Or, "Someday, when

I have self-confidence, I will get out of this raggedy relationship." Self-esteem and self-confidence are fleeting, and both can exist without radical self-love, but it almost never bodes well for anyone involved when they do. Think of all the obnoxious people you know oozing arrogance, folks we can be certain think extremely highly of themselves. Although you may call them . . . ahem . . . confident (at least that may be one of the things you call them), I bet the phrase *radical self-love* doesn't quite fit. Pick your favorite totalitarian dictator and you will likely find someone who has done just fine in the self-confidence category. After all, you would have to think you're the bee's knees to entertain the idea of single-handedly dominating the entire planet. The forty-fifth U.S. president strikes me as a man with epic self-confidence. "The Donald" is not struggling with his sense of self (even if the rest of the world is struggling with its sense of who he is). Even if we were to surmise that Trump and others like him are acting from an exaggerated lack of self-esteem or confidence, I think we can agree not much of their attitudes or actions feel like love.

You may be asking, "Okay, well if this book won't help me with my self-esteem or self-confidence, will it at least teach me self-acceptance?" My short answer is, if I do my job correctly, no! Not because self-acceptance isn't useful but because I believe there is a port far beyond the isle of self-acceptance and I want us to go there. Think back to all the times you "accepted" something and found it completely uninspiring. When I was a kid, my mother would make my brother and me frozen pot pies for dinner. It was the meal for the days she did not feel like cooking. I enjoyed the flaky pastry crust. The chunks of mechanically pressed chicken in a Band-Aid-colored beige gravy were tolerable. But there was nothing less appetizing than the abhorrent vegetable medley of peas, green beans, and carrots portioned throughout each bite like miserable stars in an endless galaxy. Yes, I ate those hateful mixed vegetables. Hunger will make you accept things. I accepted that my options were limited: pick out a million tiny peas or get a job at the ripe age of ten and figure out how to feed myself. Why am I talking about pot pies? Because self-acceptance is the mixed-veggie pot pie of radical self-love. It will keep you alive when the options are sparse, but what if there is a life beyond frozen pot pies?

Too often, *self-acceptance* is used as a synonym for *acquiescence*. We accept the things we cannot change. We accept death because we have no say over its arbitrary and indifferent arrival at our door. We have personal histories of bland acceptance. We have accepted lackluster jobs because we were broke. We have accepted lousy partners because their lousy presence was better than the hollow aloneness of their absence. We practice self-acceptance when we have grown tired of self-hatred but can't conceive of anything beyond a paltry tolerance of ourselves. What a thin coat to wear on this weather-tossed road. Famed activist and professor Angela Davis said, "I am no longer accepting the things I cannot change. I am changing the things I cannot accept."[1] We can change the circumstances that have had us settle for self-acceptance. I assure you there is a richer, thicker, cozier blanket to carry through the world. There is a realm infinitely more mind-blowing. It's called radical self-love.

> **Radical Reflection**
>
> *Concepts like self-acceptance and body neutrality are not without value. When you have spent your entire life at war with your body, these models offer a truce. But you can have more than a cease-fire. You can have radical self-love because you are already radical self-love.*

## Why the Body?

Humans are a varied and divergent bunch, with all manner of beliefs, morals, values, and ideas. We have struggled to find agreement on much of anything over the centuries (just think about how long we argued about gravity and whether the world is shaped like a pizza), but here is a completely noncontroversial statement I think we have consensus around: You, my dear, have a body. And should you desire to remain on this spinning rock hurtling through space, you will need a body to do it. Everything else we think we know is up for debate. Are we spiritual beings? Depends on who you ask. Do humans have souls? Been fighting about that since Aristotle likened the souls of fetuses to those of vegetables.[2] But bodies—yup, we got those. And given this widely agreed-upon reality, it seems to me if ever there were a place where the practice of radical love could be a transformative force, the body ought to be that location.

When we speak of the ills of the world—violence, poverty, injustice—we are not speaking conceptually; we are talking about things that happen to bodies. When we say millions around the world are impacted by the global epidemic of famine, what we are saying is that millions of humans are experiencing the physical deterioration of muscle and other tissue due to lack of nutrients in their bodies. *Injustice* is an opaque word until we are willing to discuss its material reality as, for example, the three years sixteen-year-old Kalief Browder spent beaten and locked in solitary confinement in Riker's Island prison without ever being charged with a single crime. His suicide and his mother's heart attack two years later are not abstractions; they are the outcomes injustice enacted on two bodies.[3] Racism, sexism, ableism, homo- and transphobia, ageism, fatphobia are algorithms created by humans' struggle to make peace with the body. A radical self-love world is a world free from the systems of oppression that make it difficult and sometimes deadly to live in our bodies.

A radical self-love world is a world that works for every body. Creating such a world is an inside-out job. How we value and honor our own bodies impacts how we value and honor the bodies of others. Our own radical self-love reconnection is the blueprint for what author Charles Eisenstein calls *The More Beautiful World Our Hearts Know Is Possible*.[4] It is through our own transformed relationship with our bodies that we become champions for other bodies on our planet. As we awaken to our indoctrinated body shame, we feel inspired to awaken others and to interrupt the systems that perpetuate body shame and oppression against all bodies. There is a whisper we keep hearing; it is saying we must build in us what we want to see built in the world. When we act from this truth on a global scale, using the lens of the body, we usher in the transformative opportunity of radical self-love, which is the opportunity for a more just, equitable, and compassionate world for us all.

Moving from body shame to radical self-love is a road of inquiry and insight. We will need to ask ourselves tough questions from a place of grace and grounding. Together we will examine what we have come to believe about ourselves, our bodies, and the world we live in. At times, the road may appear dark and ominous, but fret not, my friend! I have provided some lampposts along the way. They come in the form of Unapologetic Inquiries, questions you will ask yourself as you endeavor to comb the recesses of your body shame and dismantle its parts. Radical Reflections will highlight central themes and concepts you will want to remember as we take this journey together. This is not a math test and you cannot fail. Be patient with yourself, take your time. As my best friend Maureen Benson says, "You are not late."[5]

## Why Must It Be Radical?

"Okay, Sonya. I get it. Loving ourselves is important. But why do we have to be all radical about it?" To answer this question is to further distinguish radical self-love from its fickle cousins, self-confidence and self-esteem, or its scrappy kid sister, self-acceptance. It requires that we explore the definition of the word *radical*. Language is fluid and evolutionary, regularly leaving dictionary definitions feeling dated and sorely lacking in nuance. How we construct language is an enormous part of how we understand and judge bodies. The definition of *radical* is a powerful one as we explore its relationship to self-love. Dictionary.com defines *radical* as:

1. of or going to the root or origin; fundamental: a radical difference.
2. thoroughgoing or extreme, especially as regards change from accepted or traditional forms: a radical change in the policy of a company.
3. favoring drastic political, economic, or social reforms: radical ideas; radical and anarchistic ideologues.
4. forming a basis or foundation.
5. existing inherently in a thing or person: radical defects of character.[6]

Radical self-love is deeper, wider, and more expansive than anything we would call self-confidence or self-esteem. It is juicer than self-acceptance. Including the word *radical* offers us a self-love that is the root or origin of our relationship to ourselves. We did not start life in a negative partnership with our bodies. I have never seen a toddler lament the size of their thighs, the squishiness of their bellies. Children do not arrive here ashamed of their race, gender, age, or disabilities. Babies love their bodies! Each discovery they encounter is freaking awesome. Have you ever seen an infant realize they have feet? Talk about wonder! That is what an unobstructed relationship with our bodies looks like. You were an infant once, which means there was a time when you thought your body was freaking awesome too. Connecting to that memory may feel as distant as the furthest star. It may not be a memory you can access at all, but just knowing that there was a point in your history when you once loved your body can be a reminder that body shame is a fantastically crappy inheritance. We didn't give it to ourselves, and we are not obligated to keep it. We arrived on this planet as LOVE.

We need not do anything other than turn on a television for evidence affirming how desperately our society, our world, needs an extreme form of self-love to counter the constant barrage of shame, discrimination, and body-based oppression enacted against us daily. Television shows like *The Biggest Loser* encourage dangerous and unsustainable exercise and food restriction from their contestants while using their bodies as fodder for our entertainment and reinforcing the notion that the most undesirable body one can have is a fat body. Researchers have shown that American news outlets regularly exaggerate crime rates, including a tendency to inflate the rates of Black offenses while depicting Black suspects in a less favorable light than their White counterparts.[7] People with disabilities are virtually nonexistent on television unless they are being trotted out as "inspiration porn." Their stories are often told in ways that exploit their disabilities for the emotional edification of able-bodied people, presenting them as superhuman for doing unspectacular things like reading or going to the store or, worse yet, for overcoming obstacles placed on them by the very society that fails to acknowledge or appropriately accommodate their bodies.[8] *Of course* we need something radical to challenge these messages.

Using the term *radical* elevates the reality that our society requires a drastic political, economic, and social reformation in the ways in which we deal with bodies and body difference. The U.S. Constitution was written to sanction governmental body oppression. When the Bill of Rights was signed, relatively few Americans had voting rights.[9] Among those excluded from suffrage were African Americans, Native Americans, women, White men with disabilities, and White males who did not own land. Voting rights for women . . . nope. Blacks . . . nope; they were only counted as three-fifths of a full person. Using a wheelchair? No voting for you, dear. Race, gender, and disability prejudice were written into the governing documents of the United States.[10] Consider that the right to marry the person you love regardless of your gender was only legally sanctioned in the United States in 2015.[11] In certain other nations (e.g., Australia), it is still illegal.[12] Marriage equality for same-sex couples is in its historical infancy in the United States and nonexistent for most of the world. Transgender people are currently fighting across the United States to retain the legal right to use the bathroom that matches their gender identity.[13] People with disabilities have higher rates of unemployment regardless of educational attainment.[14]

These political, economic, and social issues are about our bodies. They intersect with our race, age, gender, ability, sexual orientation, and a multitude of other ways our bodies exist. In 1989 Columbia law professor and scholar Kimberlé Crenshaw gave a name to this long-understood dynamic. She called it *intersectionality* and defined it as:

> . . . the study of overlapping or intersecting social identities and related systems of oppression, domination, or discrimination. The theory suggests that—and seeks to examine how—various biological, social, and cultural categories such as gender, race, class, ability, sexual orientation, religion, caste, age, and other axes of identity interact on multiple and often simultaneous levels. The theory proposes that we should think of each element or trait of a person as inextricably linked with all of the other elements in order to fully understand one's identity.[15]

*Intersectionality* has become a term often revered or repudiated depending on the source. Put plainly, none of us are monodimensional. We are not only men, fathers, people with living with lupus, Asian, or seniors. Some of us are aging Asian fathers who are living with lupus. Those varying identities impact each other in ways that are significantly different than if we were navigating them one at a time. Radical self-love demands that we see ourselves and others in the fullness of our complexities and intersections and that we work to create space for those intersections. As has been true throughout history, changing the systemic and structural oppressions that regard us in perfunctory and myopic ways requires sweeping changes in our laws, policies, and social norms. Creating a world of justice for all bodies demands that we be radical and intersectional.

### Unapologetic Inquiry #1

*We all live at multiple intersections of identity. What are your intersections? How do your multiple identities affect each other?*

Radical self-love is interdependent. The radical self-love espoused in this book lives beyond the flimsy ethos of individualism and operates at both the individual and systemic levels. Radical self-love is about the self because the self is part of the whole. And therefore, radical self-love is the foundation of radical human love. Our relationships with our own bodies inform our relationships with others. Consider all the times you have assessed your value or lack thereof by comparing yourself to someone else. When we are saddled with body shame, we see other bodies as things to covet or judge. Body shame makes us view bodies in narrow terms like "good" or "bad," or "better" or "worse" than our own. Radical self-love invites us to love our bodies in a way that transforms how we understand and accept the bodies of others. This is not to say that we magically like everyone. It simply means we have debates and disagreements about ideas and character, not about bodies. When we can see the obvious truth inherent in body activist Hanne Blank's quote, "There is no wrong way to have a body," we learn to love bodies even when we don't like the humans inhabiting them.[16]

### Unapologetic Inquiry #2

*Can you recall an occasion when you compared yourself to someone? How did the comparison impact your self-esteem and self-confidence? How did it impact your ideas about the other person?*

Radical self-love is indeed our inherent natural state, but social, political, and economic systems of oppression have distanced us from that knowing. Remember that toddler I mentioned a few paragraphs ago who delighted in their wondrous body—a.k.a. you as a kid? I know radical self-love can seem like a planet outside any galaxy you've heard of. I want to assure you: Radical self-love is not light years away. It is not away at all. It lives in you. It is your very essence. You do not have to become radical self-love. You don't have to try to travel to it as though it were some far-off destination. Think of body shame like the layers of an onion. For decades in our own lives and for centuries in civilization, we have been taught to judge and shame our bodies and to consequently judge and shame others. Getting to our inherent state of radical self-love means peeling away those ancient, toxic messages about bodies. It is like returning the world's ugliest shame sweater back to the store where it was purchased and coming out wearing nothing but a birthday suit of radical self-love. By refusing to accept body shame as some natural consequence of being in a body, we can stop apologizing for our bodies and erase the distance between ourselves and radical self-love. When we do that we are instantly returned to the radically self-loving stars we always were. Talk about a transformative power!

## What Have We Been Apologizing For?
## What If We Stopped?

As a nine-year-old, I was sorry for everything. "Sonie, you left the refrigerator open!" "Sorry." "Sonya, why is your coat on the couch?" "Sorry." "Sonya, did you get grape jelly on that white pantsuit I paid good money for?" "Sorry, sorry, sorry . . ." A litany of apologies for my ever clumsy, messy, forgetful self, who spilled evidence of such all over the house. "Sorry" was my way of gathering up the spill. After all, I was a new generation of "raising kids" my grandmother was enlisted to do after having already raised three children on her own. I knew that my grandmother loved me, but even at nine years old I also knew she had to be exhausted. Grandma eventually started scolding me for saying *sorry* all the time. "Hush all that *sorry*. You ain't sorry. If you were sorry you would stop doing it!" I wondered if there was any truth to my grandmother's admonishment. If I were sorry, truly sorry, would I stop doing whatever *it* was? Could I?

Living in a female body, a Black body, an aging body, a fat body, a body with mental illness is to awaken daily to a planet that expects a certain set of apologies to already live on our tongues. There is a level of "not enough" or "too much" sewn into these strands of difference. Recent discoveries in the field of epigenetics have established how the traumas and resiliency of our ancestors are passed on to us molecularly.[17] Being sorry is literally a lesson in our DNA. In the Jim Crow South, an apology could at times be exacted by death sentence. Emmett Till's family came to know this brutal fact in the summer of 1955, when the fifteen-year-old's obligatory apology for whistling at a White woman would come in the form of a fatal gunshot after which his lifeless body was affixed to a tire and dumped in the Tallahatchie River.[18] For far too many women, the expectation of apology began after the sexual-assault report ended in an interrogation about the length of the skirt she was wearing or how many drinks she had at the party. There are minuscule daily ways each of us will be asked to apologize for our bodies, no matter how "normal" they appear. The conservative haircut needed to placate the new supervisor, the tattoo you cover when you step into an office building to increase your chances of being treated "professionally" are examples of tiny apologies society will ask you to render for being in your body as you see fit. For so many of us, *sorry* has become how we translate the word *body*.

## Unapologetic Inquiry #3

*In what ways have you been asked to apologize for your body?*

For decades, I spread out before the world a buffet of apologies. I apologized for laughing too loudly, being too big, too dark, flamboyant, outspoken, analytical. I watched countless others roll out similar scrolls of contrition. We made these apologies because our bodies had disabilities and needed access. We made them because our bodies were aging and slower, because our gender identity was different than the sex we were assigned at birth and it confused strangers. We apologized for our weight, race, sexual orientation. We were told there is a right way to have a body, and our apologies reflected our indoctrination into that belief. We believed there was indeed a way in which our bodies were wrong. Not only have we been trying to change our "wrong bodies" but we have also continued to apologize for the presumed discomfort our bodies rouse in others. Whether we perceived ourselves as making the passenger beside us uncomfortable by taking up "too much" space in our airplane seat or we believed that our brown skin frightened the White woman who clutched her purse and crossed the street when she saw us approaching, either way it was in these moments that we found our heads bowed in shame, certain that our too fat, too dark, too muchness was the offense. It is never the failure of the seat or of its makers, who opted not to design it for myriad bodies. Of course, it is not our media companies' exaggeration of crime in communities of color that is culpable for planting the seeds of prejudice in so many citizens. We, at every turn, have decided that we are the culprits of our own victimization. However, not only are we constantly atoning; we have demanded our fair share of apologies from others as well. We, too, have snickered at the fat body at the beach, shamed the transgender body at the grocery store, pitied the disabled body while clothes shopping, maligned the aging body. We have demanded the apology from other bodies. We have ranked our bodies against the bodies of others, deciding they are greater or lesser than our own based on the prejudices and biases we inherited.

Dismantling the culture of apology requires an investigation into the anatomy of an apology. Generally, people committed to their righteousness rarely feel the need to apologize. About five years ago I shared with an ex how something he'd said had hurt my feelings. After twenty minutes of his danc-

> **Radical Reflection**
> *Our freedom from body shame demands that we look at how we have perpetuated shame in others. We will need to be radically honest on this journey.*

ing around any admission of offense, it became clear this guy was not planning to issue any apologies. According to his logic, he did not intend to hurt my feelings and therefore did not owe me an apology. Like many people, he felt that his intention should have absolved him from his impact. I countered his reasoning by asking, "If you accidentally stepped on someone's foot, would you say *sorry*?" "No, not if their foot was the only place to stand," he replied matter-of-factly. (Why had I dated this guy?) Clearly, I do not propose that we, as a species, adopt this sort of thoughtless, self-centered ideology, but sometimes even jerks can lead us to epiphanies. There was something about his refusal to apologize for what he saw as taking up the space he needed that, if wielded authentically, might change how we move through the world. Why are we consistently apologizing for the space we inhabit? What if we all understood the inherent vastness of our humanity and therefore occupied the world without apology? What if we all became committed to the idea that no one should have to apologize for being a human in a body? What if we made room for every body so that no one ever had to stand on someone else's foot? How might we change our lives? How might we change the world?

The planet is a big, daunting place. It is easy to feel at the whim of the universe. We have been convinced we are ineffectual at exacting any real change against our social systems and structures, so instead we land the guilt and blame squarely on the shoulders of the most accessible party: ourselves. This burden has kept us immobile in our own lives and oblivious to our impact in the world. The weight of the shame has kept us small and trapped in the belief that our bodies and our lives are mistakes. What an exhausting and disheartening way to live. It was this sense of epic discouragement that fueled my inquiry into the nature of apology and led me to explore how our lives might look different if we began living unapologetically. What would the world look like if each of us navigated our lives with the total awareness that we owed no one an apology for our bodies? That exploration into unapologetic living led me to a two-tiered hypothesis. My hunch was, the more unapologetically I showed up in my body, in my community, my job, family, and world, one of two things would happen: either I would pass on to others the power and permission to be their unapologetic selves, or others would feel indicted and intimidated by my unapologetic being and would attempt to contain or shrink me. As the universe often does, it gave me the opportunity to test my hypothesis, in this case on the evening of February 9, 2011.

Six months prior, I had taken a camera-phone picture of myself in a black, strapless corset while getting dressed for an event. I was being saucy, sexy, and silly, and I absolutely did not think a single soul besides myself would ever lay eyes on that photo. For months, I'd catch myself skimming through images of old meals, museum visits, cute shoe fantasy purchases, and then I would happen upon the photo of my dark, wide body in the black corset. Damn, I was hot! And yet, despite feeling vibrant and bold, I was terrified to share the photo with anyone. The voices of apology immediately began a chorus of questions: Would people think I was vain? Would they fail to see the beautiful woman I saw in the image and instead simply remind me that I was too fat, too black, too queer, too woman, and no one was ever going to think that was beautiful? Unable to answer my litany of shame-based interrogations, the photo remained secreted away in my cell phone, only spied when I needed an esteem boost (see how my self-esteem was floating at sea, buoyed only by a selfie).

A war I could not yet name was raging inside me. It was the war between radical self-love and body shame. On February 9, 2011, a friend posted a picture of plus-size model Tara Lynn on my Facebook wall. Immediately I was taken aback by her gorgeousness and more than a little enamored (read: total crush). Searching her name on Google (a.k.a. internet stalking

> **Radical Reflection**
>
> *The voice of doubt, shame, and guilt blaring in our heads is not our voice. It is a voice we have been given by a society steeped in shame. It is the "outside voice." Our authentic voice, our "inside voice," is the voice of radical self-love!*

her) returned photo after photo of this stunning woman posing casually in jeans and a crisp white shirt for a trendy department store or wearing nothing but a string of pearls while splayed across a fur rug. But the final photo would be the one to prove at least a portion of my hypothesis. I ran the mouse across the hyperlink, and there was Tara

Lynn standing resplendent in a black corset, the cover girl for a new lingerie campaign.[19] Her empowered being instantly empowered my being. In one click of a digital image, Tara Lynn gave me permission to be fully seen in my body, opinions be damned! I did in that moment what I had felt completely incapable of doing for months: I immediately posted the picture of me in my black corset to Facebook. Alongside the image I wrote the following caption: "In this picture, I am 230lbs. In this picture, I have stretch marks and an unfortunate decision in the shape of a melting Hershey's kiss on my left thigh. I am smiling, like a woman who knows you're watching and likes it. For this one camera flash, I am unashamed, unapologetic."[20]

Just as Tara Lynn's unapologetic power permissioned my own, I did the same for others, asking my friends to share photos in which they felt unashamed and unapologetic in their bodies. The next morning I opened my Facebook page only to discover I had been tagged in over thirty photos of people of varying ages, races, sizes, abilities, genders, sexual orientations, and more who had chosen, even if just for that brief minute, to stop hiding and apologizing and instead simply be their unabashed selves. I was consumed. I needed to know the bounds of this unmapped universe where all of us could live in our bodies like we knew we were already okay. Aware that I would need other unapologetic people willing to explore this budding notion with me, I did what any Gen Xer on the cusp of Millennial status would do: I started a Facebook group and used it to house these newly sourced unapologetic photos from my friends around the country. The group operated as a geographically unconstrained space where we could practice loving ourselves, our bodies, and other people's bodies unapologetically. I named the page after a poem I had written right around the time I took that fateful saucy selfie: "The Body Is Not an Apology." Quickly it became clear that our brief moments of unapologetic living were highly contagious acts—like the flu, but much happier!

Being unapologetic created an opening for radical self-love. Each time we chose to embrace the fullness of ourselves, some layer of the body-shame onion got peeled away, evidencing the power of every small unapologetic act. I have been watching this radical disrobing of shame change the world, one unapologetic human at a time. And each moment that I practice living unapologetically I realize my grandma was right: I wasn't ever actually sorry. When we truly love ourselves, there is no need to be.

### Unapologetic Inquiry #4

*What are you ready to stop apologizing for?*

## The Three Peaces

From the moment the phrase "The body is not an apology" and the idea of radical self-love fell from my lips, they have echoed as a re-sounding "Yes!" to those who have heard them. That YES feeling is likely the reason you are reading this book right now. On some cel-lular level, we know our bodies are not something we should apolo-gize for. After all, they are the only way we get to experience this ridiculous and radiant life. A part of us is a bit repelled by the overt espousal of body shame. It is the reason we whisper and rumor about other folks' bodies behind their backs. We know our snickers and taunts are wrong. When we are honest with ourselves, we feel gross about the way we vulture other humans, picking apart their bodies, consuming them for the sake of our own fragile sense of self. We feel gross when we think about all the vicious, cruel comments we've heard leveled against people's bodies, comments spoken around us without a single protest from us.

Our best selves find the evisceration of other humans repugnant. We feel shame when we are shamed. And when we allow ourselves, we feel shame for having shamed others. Feelings of shame suck! So what do we do? Stop shaming people? No. We distance ourselves from the guilt by couching our body judgment in the convenient container of choice. We say things like, "Hey, it's okay to judge them, they chose to be gay." "You know you could lose weight if you wanted to!" "It's not my fault you are a guy dressing like a girl!"

The argument that people "chose" to be this way or the other is at its core an argument about difference and our inability to understand and make peace with difference. The notion of choice is a convenient scapegoat for our bias and bigotries. Logic says, "If people are choosing to be different, they can just as simply choose to be the way I believe they should be." What we must ask ourselves instead is, "Why do I need people to be the way I believe they should be?" The argument about choice is a projection. There are endless things in the world we do not understand, and yet we live in a culture where we are expected to know and understand everything! Humans are rarely given permission to not understand without someone calling us failures or stupid. No one wants to feel like a stupid failure, and our brains have all sorts of nifty tricks to avoid those feelings.

A particularly strategic maneuver is to decide that if we don't understand something it must be wrong. After all, wrong is simpler than not knowing. Wrong means I am not stupid or failing. See all that sneaky, slimy projection happening there? Projection shields us from personal responsibility. It obscures our shame and confusion and places the onus for reconciling it on the body of someone else. We don't have to work to understand something when it is someone else's "fault." We don't have to undo the shame-based beliefs we were brought up with. We don't have to question our parents, friends, churches, synagogues, mosques, government, media. We don't have to challenge or be challenged. When we decide that people's bodies are wrong because we don't understand them, we are trying to avoid the discomfort of divesting from an entire body-shame system.

How do we fight the impetus to make the bodies we do not understand wrong? There are three key tenets that will help pry us out of the mire of body judgment and shame. I call them the Three Peaces. They are:

1. Make peace with not understanding.
2. Make peace with difference.
3. Make peace with *your* body.

## Peace with Not Understanding

We must make peace with not understanding. Understanding is not a prerequisite for honor, love, or respect. I know very little about the stars, but I honor their beauty. I know virtually nothing about black holes, but I respect their incomprehensible power. I do not understand the shelf life of Twinkies, but I love them and pray there be an endless supply in the event of an apocalypse! When we liberate ourselves from the expectation that we must have all things figured out, we enter a sanctuary of empathy. Being uncertain, lacking information or simply not knowing something ought not be an indictment against our intelligence or value. Lots of exceptionally smart people can't work a copy machine. This is not about smarts. Nor am I proposing we eschew information. Quite to the contrary, this is an invitation to curiosity. Not knowing is an opportunity for exploration without judgment and demands. It leaves room for the possibility that we might conduct all manner of investigation, and after said research is completed we may still not "get it." Whatever "it" may be. Understanding is ideal, but it is not an essential ingredient for making peace. Buddhist teachings tell us that the alleviation of suffering is achieved through the act of acceptance.[21] Here is a place where acceptance becomes a tool of expansion. Genuine acceptance invites reality without resistance. Wrong and right are statements of resistance and are useless when directed at people's bodies. "Her thin body is just wrong" sounds nonsensical because beneath our many layers of body shame, we know that bodies are neither wrong nor right. They just are.

Acceptance should not be confused with compliance or the proposal that we must be resigned to the ills and violence of the world. We should not. But we must be clear that people's bodies are not the cause of our social maladies. Napoleon was not a tyrant because he was short. Osama bin Laden was not a terrorist because Muslims are predisposed to violence. Our disconnection, trauma, lack of resources, lack of compassion, fear, greed, and ego are the sources of our contributions to human suffering, not our bodies. We can accept humans and their bodies without understanding "why" they love, think, move, or look the way they do. Contrary to common opinion, freeing ourselves from the need to understand everything can bring about a tremendous amount of peace.

---

### Unapologetic Inquiry #5

*What are you willing to stop struggling to understand for the sake of peace?*

---

## Peace with Difference

We must make peace with difference. This is a simple perspective when applied to nature, but oh, how we struggle when transferring the concept onto human forms. The late poet and activist Audre Lorde said, "It is not our differences that divide us. It is our inability to recognize, accept, and celebrate those differences."[22] Think of all the times we have heard some well-meaning person attempting to usher in social harmony by declaring, "But aren't we all the same?" Here's the short answer to that: No. We are not all the same, no more than every tree is the same or every houseplant or dog. Humans are a complicated and varied bunch, and those variations impact our lived experiences. The idea that we are all the same is often a mask. It is what we tell ourselves when we haven't mastered the first Peace. Rather than owning that we don't understand someone's experience, we shrink it or stuff it into our tiny capsules of knowledge. We homogenize it by proclaiming we are all the same.

Dr. Deb Burgard, a renowned eating disorders therapist and pioneer in the Health at Every Size (HAES)[23] movement, co-created a brilliant animated video called "The Danger of Poodle Science" to explain body diversity and the perils of assessing health and wellness based on assumptions about size.[24] In it, Dr. Burgard details how absurd it would be if we assessed the health of all dogs by comparing them to the size and health of poodles. Better yet, what if the poodles decided that all other dogs should look, eat, and be the same size as poodles? The video pokes fun at our medical industry and its one-size-fits-all orientation toward bodies. Rather than acknowledging and basing research on the premise that diversity in weight and size are natural occurrences in humans, we treat larger bodies with poodle science and then pathologize those bodies by using the rhetoric of health. "I just want this complete stranger, whose life I know nothing about and who I have made no effort to get to know beyond this Twitter thread, to be healthy." This is called health trolling or concern trolling, and it is just another sinister body shame tactic. Given that we can make no accurate assessment of any individual's health based simply on their weight (or photo on social media), it is evident that such behavior is not really about the person's health but more likely about the ways in which we expect other bodies to conform to our standards and beliefs about what a body should or should not look like. Equally damaging is our insistence that all bodies should be healthy. Health is not a state we owe the world. We are not less valuable, worthy, or loveable because we are not healthy. Lastly, there is no standard of health that is achievable for all bodies. Our belief that there should be anchors the systemic oppression of ableism and reinforces the notion that people with illnesses and disabilities have defective bodies rather than different bodies. Each of us will have varying degrees of health and wellness throughout our lives and our arbitrary demands and expectations as it relates to the health and size of people's bodies fuels inequality and injustice. Quite simply, everyone is not a poodle, and that is okay. Boy would the world be a boring, yappy place if we all were.

Bodies are diverse, not only in size but in race and ethnicity, sexual orientation, gender, physical ability, and mental health. The example of poodle science speaks to a larger issue, one in which our societies have defined what is considered a "normal" body and have assigned greater value, resources, and opportunities to the bodies most closely aligned with those ideas of "normal." When we propose that all bodies are the same, we also propose that there is a standard to measure sameness against. I call this standard the "default body."

Aspects of the default body change across culture and geography, but it shapes our ideas of normalcy and impacts our social values. We will explore later how our notions of default bodies developed over time, but for now just know that our propensity to shrink human diversity into sameness creates exhausting barriers for the bodies that do not fit our default models. We must move from occasionally

> **Radical Reflection**
> *"Celebrating difference" is nice but not transformative. It is constrained by the boundaries of our imaginations. We must strive to create a difference-celebrating culture where we see diversity as an intrinsic part of our everyday lives.*

celebrating difference (as long as it doesn't fall too far outside the boundaries of our ideas of "normal") to developing a difference-celebrating culture. Inequality and injustice rest firmly on our unwillingness to exalt the vast magnificence of the human body.

> ## Unapologetic Inquiry #6
>
> *In what ways have you tried to make other people "the same" as you? What parts of their identity did you erase by doing this?*

## Peace with Your Body

Lastly, you must make peace with *your* body. I have been talking all kumbaya and collective in the first two Peaces, but this one is all on you, love. Your body is the body it is. Your belief that your body should be some other body other than the body it is, is likely a reflection of your struggles with the first two Peaces. As I said at the beginning of the book, you did not come to the planet hating your body. What if you accepted the fact that much of how you view your body and your judgments of it are learned things, messages you have deeply internalized that have created an adversarial relationship? Hating your body is like finding a person you despise and then choosing to spend the rest of your life with them while loathing every moment of the partnership. I know that lots of humans stay in loveless commitments. Not only am I proposing that you should not stay in a loveless partnership; I am also proposing that your partner has been set up. If your body were an episode of *Law and Order: Special Victims Unit,* it would be getting framed for crimes it did not commit. Get out of that damn television show and into living in peace and harmony with the body you have today. Your body need not be a prison sentence. And if you are living in it as such, I am glad you picked up this book. As they say in the tradition of twelve-step programs, "You are in the right place."[25]

I am not simply proposing that you make peace with your body because your body shame is making you miserable. I am proposing you do it because it's making us miserable too. Your children are sad that they have no photos with you. Your teenager is wondering if they, too, will be obligated to hate their body because they see you hating yours. The bodies you share space with are afraid you are judging them with the same venom they have watched you use to judge yourself. Remember that body shame is as contagious as radical self-love. Making peace with your body is your mighty act of revolution. It is your contribution to a changed planet where we might all live unapologetically in the bodies we have.

### Unapologetic Inquiry #7

*Who in your life is most affected by your body shame? How is it impacting them?*

I know you may be saying, "But I don't know how to make peace with my body!" On these pages, together, we are going to help you master the third Peace. The key to getting out of a maze is remembering the way you got in. It's not an easy task, but this book is an attempt to start at the beginning and show you how you got to the center of body shame. Together we are going to walk back to the beginning and out of the maze. Radical self-love is both the light that will guide us and the gift on the other side.

### Radical Reflection

*Spend some time reflecting on Chapter 1. Notice what fears or concerns it triggers in you. Notice where there is excitement or joy. Share both with a friend.*

# 2

# Shame, Guilt, and Apology— Then and Now

## When Did We Learn to Hate Them?

"Keisha Bald Spots!" was the consistent choral offering on Keisha's brief bus ride to Woolslair Elementary School. The teasing was brutal and regular, but in some ways the daily routine made it easier to adapt to. Keisha's mama had a penchant for gorgeous, labyrinthine braided hairstyles. Her mother also had the grip of an X-Men character, and by the time Keisha was in third grade the tight braids had ripped her hair right out of her nine-year-old scalp, causing permanent bald spots on both sides of her head, a condition known as traction alopecia. Being different is difficult in a world that tells us there is a "normal." Many of us have oriented our entire lives around an effort to be "normal," never realizing that "normal" is not a stationary goal. It keeps moving while we dance a perpetual foxtrot, jitterbug, and paso doble around it, trying to catch up and confused when we finish each day exhausted and uninspired by this party called life.

It is considered normal for women and girls in the United States to have hair, a reality shaped to varying degrees by the default of

Westernized beauty standards. In Western societies hair is often tied
to notions of femininity, beauty, and gender. Having hair is what is
expected of a "normal" woman or girl. Of course, there is an endless
screed of rules governing our notions of normal hair. One cannot have
too much hair or too little. Hair can only be in certain places on our
bodies. Hair should have a certain texture, should be a certain color.
For Americans, the rules for hair (like most of our body rules) come
with a default aesthetic: long, straight, fine . . . and, if possible, blonde.

Even before the children on the school bus began singing "Keisha! Keisha Bald Spots!" it is likely that Keisha already knew she did
not fit the default of normal hair. Commercials would have told her,
music would have said it, pictures in her school books would have
made it clear that Keisha's hair was not the default. Her short, dark,
kinky hair and soon-to-be-partially-bald head would never be the default and by extension never normal. In our society, normal is the
pathway to worthy and beautiful.

## Body-Shame Origin Stories

If I asked you to recall your first memory of body shame, it is likely
that your story, like Keisha's, would have at least one of the following
elements:

- Developed in your youth
- Was a response to rapid or unexpected body change
- Occurred when you became aware of difference
- Led you to assume there was some "should" about your body
- Was reflected or reinforced by familial, social, cultural, and
  political messaging
- Was attached to a story or belief about your value and worth
  in the world

Having travelled the country and listened to thousands of body-
shame stories, I observed patterns that elucidated how our indoc-

trination into body shame shares some key characteristics. For many of us, our first shame memories occur before we even enter our teenage years. It is unsurprising that early on we internalize these negative messages. Being young and particularly impressionable, we take cues from the external world about who we are and who we should be. In childhood, when we are highly impressionable and in the infancy of developing a sense of individuation and identity, it is no surprise that the earliest seeds of body shame might begin to take root. A Yahoo Health survey of 1,993 teen and adult respondents found that the average age of body-shame consciousness was between thirteen and fourteen. Additionally, it found that respondents were experiencing body shame at increasingly younger ages, some beginning at nine and ten.[1] In the workshops on radical self-love offered by The Body Is Not an Apology, participants are asked to share their earliest memories of body shame.[2] Here are some responses:

> *I was around seven years old and a little boy in school, named James, called me fat. I think that was when I started dieting.*
>
> ~KATHLEEN

> *At about age seven, the older brother of a friend told me girls couldn't go topless because it was dirty.*
>
> ~EMMA

> *I was four years old, my first day at daycare, and a little boy [told] me I looked like a bulldog.*
>
> ~AMY

For Amy, Kathleen, Emma, and Keisha, those early messages stuck with them and shaped their sense of worth and value. The messages altered how they felt about their bodies. Girls are by no means the only ones receiving these detrimental messages. Boys, trans children, and gender-nonconforming children receive similar shaming messages in their early years.[3]

> *I was twelve years old when my basketball teammates and*
> *I were changing in the locker room. One of the kids called*
> *me chicken chest because I was so skinny. My team made*
> *clucking noises at me for the rest of the season.*
>
> ~DAVID

> *From the age of six I knew I felt like a boy. I hated the*
> *dresses and dolls my mother forced on me. Whenever*
> *I complained, she'd tell me as long as she bought the clothes,*
> *I would wear what she told me to. I learned quickly that*
> *who I was, was not okay.*
>
> ~ALEX

---

### Unapologetic Inquiry #8

*What is your earliest memory of body shame? How is it similar to or different from the other stories shared here?*

---

Our seminal experiences of body shame are often a result of some rapid or noticeable change in our physical selves. Nia was my childhood playmate and neighbor who lived in the same court of townhouses in East Liberty, a working-class neighborhood in my hometown of Pittsburgh, Pennsylvania. Nia was a few years older than the rest of the kids on my block and the first to be visited by the puberty fairy. On a sweaty July afternoon, while Nia, I, and several of the neighborhood kids beat the midday pavement in a rousing game of red light/green light, the adults were loudly scrutinizing our clumsy, gangly child bodies. Looking us over with equal parts marvel and pity, my two aunts and Nia's mother demanded, "Nia, come here. Are those bee stings, Nia?" My eldest aunt snickered. "Yup, looks like she's been stung," my younger aunt cackled. "Mmm-hmm, she been stung, and I just don't know what I am gonna do with her now!" chided her mother. My ten-year-old self was seriously confused. Why wasn't Nia crying after being stung by a bee? I always cried when that happened. Was it a special bee that didn't hurt? And even more confusing were the adults. Why were the grown folks laughing at her and being weird instead of helping her? Within moments it clicked. No one was discussing an insect-inflicted injury; they were poking fun at Nia's . . . gasp . . . boobies! Ten-year-old Sonya was mortified! Of course, if I could figure out this not-so-inside joke, certainly the eight other kids milling about would be in on the comedy soon enough. And my God, would this be what happened to me when I got the dreaded bee stings? In a mere five minutes, I had run through every embarrassing disaster scenario my puberty might elicit from the surrounding adults, all while poor Nia fled the scene, retreating to her home. I saw Nia just a few times the rest of the summer. I think she was hiding. From that moment forward, puberty became synonymous with public

> ### Radical Reflection
> *Children's bodies are not public property. Teaching children bodily autonomy, privacy, and consent are the cornerstones of raising radical self-love humans.*

humiliation. I learned that our bodies and their changes were areas of public domain—and things to broadcast, be teased about, be ashamed of.

Can you recall the messages you received about your own rapidly changing body during puberty? For all its everydayness, puberty is hard when you are a kid, even for those of us with experiences the world might call "normal." To understand the scope and range of body shame, we must consider what navigating the already treacherous terrain of rapid body change might be like for bodies that do not fit the definition of normal. What of the child whose gender identity does not match the changes their body is experiencing during puberty? What of the child navigating puberty in a fat body or a body with chronic illness? Our experiences of body shame are layered upon and impacted by the intersections of our identities. The less "normal" our identity, the more fraught the waters of body shame. Research shows that nearly 50 percent of transgender youth have seriously thought about suicide, and 25 percent report that they have made a suicide attempt.[4] How we are treated during puberty can be not only life-altering but life-threatening for some young people. As we consider our own body-shame origin story, we have potent access to a deeper empathy for all bodies.

Body shame is often a result of our burgeoning consciousness about our own difference. Whew, we sure do have a long-standing battle with our difference. Our first encounter with noticing our difference might have been when Billy in second grade pointed out that we had the biggest schnozzle . . . ahem . . . nose in the class. Maybe that consciousness came into focus with the awareness of our racial or sexual identities. Humans struggle with that second Peace. Part of our evolutionary success can be attributed to our skill at quickly assessing danger. "Nope, that is not a person; that is a boa constrictor!" See, quick! In an evolutionary sense, humans' ability to discern difference assured that we stayed near the top of the food chain. Whereas noticing difference was historically necessary, modern humans have continued to use difference to sort ourselves, conflating difference with danger. Our rapid assessment of difference can be understood through a psychosocial dynamic called "in-group out-group bias." In 1982, researcher Henry Tajfel divided people into two random groups. He found that people began to favor their random group over people in the other random group (emphasis on *random*), at times even rationalizing reasons for the other group's immorality or poor character to justify disliking them.[5] Our ancient ancestors' battles for resources, food, even mates ensured that humans needed to find ways to identify who was part of their tribe and who was not. This in-group out-group distinction also meant that those outside our group were seen as a threat to our resources. Ultimately we are wired to recognize difference and maybe even distrust it. However, we were also wired to eat bugs and to poop in a hole in the ground. The point being, we are capable of change. Seeing difference as synonymous with danger is an aspect of our social evolution that can and should be shifted. But we must grapple with difference. Our attempts to mute it reinforce the idea that difference is inherently bad.

## Unapologetic Inquiry #9

*When was the first time you noticed that you or someone else was different? What did you make the difference mean about you? What did you make it mean about them?*

A year or so ago, a woman in one of my workshops shared that as a darker-skinned Black ballerina, she felt, from early in her training, as if something were holding her back. Eventually she concluded that it was the color of her skin. What might make this young woman feel as if her Blackness was a disadvantage in her pursuits as a classical dancer? Consider this hypothesis: when we don't see ourselves reflected in the world around us, we make judgments about that absence. Invisibility is a statement. It says something about the world and our place in it. A 2014 MTV study done in collaboration with David Binder Research found that among Millennials, 73 percent of respondents believed that never considering race would improve society.[6] Unfortunately, despite our dreams of a utopic, color-blind planet, this thinking only functions to reinforce body shame. How many times have we heard or said the following statement: "I don't see color"? Although well-intentioned, not seeing color is ultimately a reflection of our personal challenges around navigating difference.

We may be trying to convey how we don't judge people based on racial identity, but "color blindness" is an act of erasure. Not only does it make invisible all the experiences a person has had that were shaped by their racial identity or color; it implies that to truly respect another human being we must obscure their areas of difference. Remember that we live in a world of default bodies, the bodies we imagine when we close our eyes. The default body becomes the template for the normal body. The only reason we would need to erase someone's difference is because we still equate difference with danger or undesirability. When we say we don't see color, what we are truly saying is, "I don't want to see the things about you that are different because society has told me they are dangerous or undesirable." Ignoring difference does not change society; nor does it change the experiences non-normative bodies must navigate to survive. Rendering difference invisible validates the notion that there are parts of us that should be ignored, hidden, or minimized, leaving in place the unspoken idea that difference is the problem and not our approach to dealing with difference. Proposing that humans are all the same leaves the idea of the default body uninterrogated in our subconscious and firmly in place in our world, forcing all other bodies to conform or be rendered invisible.

### Unapologetic Inquiry #10

*Have you ever said any of the following: "I don't see color." "We are all the same." "I don't care if a person is white, black, purple or whatever." "They are playing the 'race card.'" Considering this passage, what might you say next time?*

Adults reinforce the message that different is bad by encouraging children to minimize difference or shaming them when they point it out. Diane, one of my workshop participants, recalled an incident in a grocery store when she went to pick up some vegetables for dinner. She encountered a woman and her four-year-old in the aisle directly in front of Diane's electric wheelchair. Diane was preparing to ask them to move over so that she could get to the eggplants when the woman's child began to point and squeal. Diane imagined that the child was responding not only to her apparent difference but also to her chair. The child's motioning and repetition of the phrase "Momma, it's an elecwic car!" suggested that Diane's chair perhaps looked like a toy car to the young child. All this deduction happened within a few seconds before the humiliated mother scolded the child for pointing and rushed off, never even acknowledging Diane's presence. Diane was disappointed. What could have been a powerful teaching opportunity turned into a mother reinforcing the notion that difference is not to be acknowledged. That child likely left the encounter feeling as if they had done something very wrong by openly noticing Diane. The child also left thinking that electric wheelchairs are toys. Inadvertently, the mother's actions conveyed the message that if bodies look different or move differently, we should not acknowledge that difference. This act leaves the idea of default bodies standing.

The most distressing message in Diane's encounter was the unintentional but deeply harmful one that disabled bodies should be ignored. Every message we receive as children tells us something not only about our own bodies but also about the bodies of others. How we treat difference and how we explain it to children can either reinforce the notions of body-based hierarchies or dismantle them. When we explore our assumptions about the bodies of others, we are better able to see where our defaults hinder the full range of human identity.

---

### Unapologetic Inquiry #11

*Take a moment and think about the story of Diane and the mother and child at the grocery store. Consider what defaults you may have subconsciously assigned to the people in the story. Did you racialize them? If so, what races did you make them? Did you give the child a gender? Did you assume that the mother and child were able-bodied? Did they have large or small bodies?*

---

This exploration of how we assign default bodies is connected to our origins of body shame and the formation of the dreaded *should*. Our earliest memories of body shame left us with a sense that something was wrong with us, that our bodies should be different than they were (while consequently being the same as the other bodies around us). How we decided what our bodies should look like was formed in part by the messages we received. Those messages were transmitted and reinforced by culture, society, politics, and our families. Those messages stuck with us. The website About-Face.org provides young women with the tools to challenge media messages that endanger their self-esteem and body image. The site reports that in a study of 112 female undergraduates, exposure to thin-ideal advertisements increased body dissatisfaction, negative mood, and levels of depression, and also lowered self-esteem. About-Face.org also highlighted a longitudinal study of adolescents that found frequent reading of magazine articles about dieting and/or weight loss was associated with weight-control behaviors and other psychological outcomes five years later.[7]

Confusing and stifling social messages about our bodies and identities transcend gender. Daemon, one of only a handful of male participants at my workshop, recalled his first memory of body shame at eight years old. He took a hard tumble off a merry-go-round at the local playground and scraped his knee badly. Bloodied and crying, he ran to his teenage and twenty-something cousins, who were supervising the smaller kids at the park. They immediately met his tears with laughter and taunting. The eldest cousin admonished, "Man up, dude! Only sissies cry." Daemon was clear that the brief but impactful moment changed him; he shared how he had not cried since he was eight years old. In those few brief moments, Daemon's cousins taught him that "man up" meant he must ignore both physical and emotional pain to be considered a man. His tears were bad and his pain inconsequential. Cultural and familial messages that reduce masculinity to a bland soup of physical strength and stoic emotional response limit the full range of human expression needed for boys to develop a healthy sense of radical self-love. We call these dangerous ideas "toxic masculinity."[8] Specifically, narratives that reinforce masculinity as synonymous with muscles can lead young men to "crash diets, over-exercising, smoking, increased drug and alcohol use or even taking dangerous supplements."[9] For Daemon, it led to years of ignoring his body, avoiding doctors, and masking pain with drugs and alcohol. Daemon said, "Having a stroke at thirty-seven was my wake-up call. If this was being a man, I was ready for a new definition." Cultural and social missives about who we are supposed to be and how our bodies are supposed to look are woven into the fabric of our daily lives, and whether we want to admit it or not, they impact our sense of self, often for decades to come. They become part of a larger story.

Let's return to Keisha for a moment. Can we see how the messages she received about her hair were cultural, social, and familial? Keisha recounted this story of shame in a workshop twenty-five years later, her voice still a cracked egg. I listened as she shared how she had felt unattractive and unlovable for nearly three decades, all because of her hair. It was clear that Keisha was moving through the world with her body-shame origin story still echoing against the walls of her life. She still lived in the shame of her story. The question is, In what ways are you?

## Unapologetic Inquiry #12

*How are your early memories of body shame impacting your life today? What do find yourself doing or not doing as a result of the shame?*

## Media Matters

At this point in our journey together you are likely to be experiencing one of two states. The first is a condition one of my workshop participants called "meta-shame." This is the state of feeling shame for feeling shame about our bodies. Doesn't it sound exhausting? It is!

In this blossoming age of "body positivity," it is trendy to profess our undying body love. We treat body positivity as though it is a trophy we can only receive when we reach some state of self-love enlightenment. Body shame is about as unfashionable as the rollers and bathrobe my mother would occasionally pick me up from school wearing, and yet for so many of us it is still our truth. It can be maddening when we see the ways in which we remain stuck on the carousel of our negative beliefs about default bodies and difference. We rage at ourselves about why we can't seem to crack the clay of body shame. Across the landscape of our existence we see its ravages everywhere and feel acutely conscious of all the risks we have not taken because of it. We ache for all the opportunities we have ignored. Splattered before us like bugs on the windshield of life are all the ways we have shrunk the full expression of ourselves because we have been convinced that our bodies and therefore our very beings are deficient. We can also see how our inability to get out of our shame story amplifies our feelings of inadequacy. Our presumed failure at attaining some body-love nirvana becomes just another source of shame.

The second state might involve an unexpected hankering to track down and curse Curtis from fifth grade who teased you to the point of tears. You are feeling certain he is the source of your body woes! Maybe you are blaming your mother who scolded you every time you reached for dessert after dinner. Yes! She is to blame! It is not surprising that these folks seem like malevolent perpetrators responsible for our years of body

> ### Radical Reflection
> *Avoid meta-shame, which is shame for having so much shame. Take a deep breath of kindness for yourself and your history of body shame/shaming. We can only do what we know. As famed poet Maya Angelou says, "When we know better, we do better." We can do better by giving ourselves more love.*

hatred and shame. But before you unleash the radical self-love army of vengeance upon their heads, you should know . . . there is no radical self-love army of vengeance. You should also know that although Curtis and your mother may indeed have helped you cultivate some awful beliefs about your body, they were not the authors of your body shame. Nor are you failing at body positivity. You, your mama, and Curtis have merely been pawns in a much longer and larger game of how we have all come to understand, judge, value, or devalue our bodies and the bodies of others.

Relationships with our bodies are social, political, and economic inheritances. The nature of these inheritances has changed over time, the default body morphing and transforming to suit the power structures of the day. We have not always seen fat bodies as less valuable. Throughout periods of human history, we have seen larger bodies not as markers of laziness or ill health but rather as representative of a life of wellness, wealth, and ease—something to aspire to. A larger body was representative of aristocracy and affluence. Fatness was all the rage for a while.[10] Gender and gender roles have also shifted over time, bending to fit the needs of the society. In 1503, Queen Hatshepsut ascended to the throne of Egypt while donning male clothing and a beard to symbolize her intention to rule as a pharaoh.[11] Not all cultures have seen gender through rigid assignments of male or female. Indigenous cultures around the world have long accepted the concept of "two-spirit" people: those who embody both feminine and masculine identities or whose gender is more complicated than one of two options.[12] There were periods of time in history when the constructs of race looked considerably different. Irish folks were not enfolded into Whiteness when they arrived in America; neither were the Polish or Italians.[13] These elements of our identities are socially constructed and transmitted through a multitude of vehicles, including family, community, and culture. But no vehicle has been as potent in shaping our perceptions of bodies on a global scale as the vehicle of media.

Today we turn on the television or Netflix to watch our favorite series. Listen to satellite radio as we drive to work. Read the newspaper at lunch or scroll through the headlines populating our social media timelines. The many forms of media we interact with are ubiquitous entities informing nearly every aspect of our daily lives. Their pervasiveness and our

> **Radical Reflection**
> *All our body rules are made up!*

rapid access to them seem almost like science fiction (these days, something out of a dystopian novel), but forms of mass media have always existed, merely adapting and expanding as we have evolved. The ways in which we have managed to disseminate information on a mass scale for the last century and a half evidence the power of media. The town crier: a type of media. The pony express: a form of media. Paul Revere's fateful ride, when he yelled, "The British are coming!" might have been a hashtag campaign if executed today.

Humans have always found ways to relay mass messages. The speed and distance at which these messages travel are what have changed. As the media has become a more efficient, expedient, and accessible force, its value has ballooned beyond simply being the prevailing method of disseminating information for a society. Just as importantly, it has become an economic juggernaut for the structure of global capitalism to generate wealth off our body shame—what I like to call the global Body-Shame Profit Complex (BSPC).

The earliest connection between information dissemination and revenue generation can be traced back to the first newspaper advertisement, which appeared in the *Boston Newsletter* in 1704. By the early 1900s, advertising had become its own industry and the primary source of revenue for countless newspapers.[14] Selling us things became a big deal. The arrival of radio and television exploded the possibilities of mass communication and ushered in an inexhaustible stream of potential revenue. The website EMarketer.com, which tracks global advertising spending, reported that in 2015, the worldwide advertising industry spent $513 billion to sell us pickles, rugs, brakes, beer, weight loss supplements, antiaging creams, skin lighteners, muscle supplements, plastic surgery, and tens of thousands of other completely useful and completely useless products and services.[15] We can be certain the advertisers who are spending more than half a trillion dollars per year to convince us to buy stuff are undoubtedly successful at their jobs and earning considerable profit from their efforts. However, let us not forget that advertisers are merely middlemen. They are being paid to sell industry products. If advertisers are reaping a financial boon, then the product makers are sipping Chandon from the starboard side of a yacht named the SS *Sucks to Be You*! Who are these product makers chugging pricey Prosecco? A portion of them are the profiteers of the Body-Shame Profit Complex. Earnings for the global beauty market reached an epic $460 billion in 2014, and are expected to reach $675 billion by

2020.[16] Whether we are buying hair dye to cover the greys or con-
cealer to cover the blemishes, the "beauty" sector is grossing nearly
as much money as the entire advertising industry spends, all to benefi-
cently help us have . . . ahem . . . shinier hair, fewer wrinkles, and longer lashes! Sounds like poodle-science marketing to me. To offer some
perspective, $460 billion is more than the gross domestic product of
167 nations.[17] What does this mean? Well, it means we are collec-
tively spending more on lipstick, shampoo, and tanning spray than
the entire economic infrastructure of three-fourths of the planet's
countries. It also means if we all stopped buying beauty supplies,
let's say . . . tomorrow, we would not only collapse the BSPC; we
would tank the global economy. My hunch is that unlike the banks,
we would not get a bailout!

### Unapologetic Inquiry #13

*How has body shame fueled your consumerism? What do
you buy to "be normal," "fit in," or "fix your flaws"?*

Our exploration into advertising and media is at its root a critique
of the exploitative nature of capitalism and consumerism. Our economic systems shape how we see our bodies and the bodies of
others, and they ultimately inform what we are compelled to do and
buy based on that reflection. Profit-greedy industries work with media outlets to offer us a distorted perception of ourselves and then
use that distorted self-image to sell us remedies for the distortion.
Consider that the female body type portrayed in advertising as the
"ideal" is possessed naturally by only 5 percent of American women.
Whereas the average U.S. woman is five feet four inches tall and weighs
140 pounds, the average U.S. model is five feet eleven and weighs
117. Now consider a *People* magazine survey which reported that
80 percent of women respondents said images of women on televi-

sion and in the movies made them feel insecure. Together, those statistics and those survey results illustrate a regenerative market of people who feel deficient based on the images they encounter every day, seemingly perfectly matched with advertisers and manufacturers who have just the products to sell them (us) to fix those imagined deficiencies.[18]

## Buying to Be "Enough"

A 2013 article from *InStyle* magazine reported that the average American woman spends $15,000 on beauty products over the course of her lifetime. Nearly $3,770 is spent on mascara, $2,750 on eye shadow, and $1,780 on lipstick.[19] That, my friend, is an epic amount of lipstick. If I handed you $15,000 to read this book (I *really* want folks to read this book), what would you do with it? Let me make some guesses. Pay down debt? Put a down payment on a house? Take a vacation to some exotic location? Help your children or loved ones? Go back to school? Buy an alpaca? Whether I guessed your specific answer correctly or not, I am willing to bet five million of Bill Gates's dollars that you did not say, "Sonya, I would buy a lifetime supply of antiaging cream!" I have posed this question to thousands of people across the United States and abroad, and not one person has ever replied by telling me they'd buy a lifetime supply of hair dye, liposuction, weight loss or muscle enhancing pills. No one has even said they would buy a sixty-year membership to their local 24 Hour Fitness. When given the opportunity to think about how we would spend our money if we thought of it as a powerful and abundant resource (which, by the way, it totally is), we choose things that bring us closest to the epicenter of our joy and remind us of what is central about being alive. In the depth of our hearts we know that the answers have never been liposuction, grey-hair remedies, or the loss of twenty pounds, because in the grand scheme of a life well lived, eye liner, dress sizes, and ripped abs really don't matter.

We humans are masters of distraction, using makeup, weight loss, and a finely curated self-image to avoid being present to our fears, even as they build blockades around our most potent desires. Reading a bunker's worth of blemish-cream reviews is the perfect antidote if you want to keep avoiding those annoying university applications sitting on your desk—the ones you have yet to fill out even though you promised yourself you would go back to school. Fretting about the fifteen pounds you have been fretting about for fifteen years is a lighter load than paying down the $15,000 in credit card debt so you can finally start that business you always wanted. We are not "bad" or frivolous people for buying beauty products. Nor am I proposing that lipstick or any other such purchase is innately evil. Personally, I love a good MAC shade. (Film Noir is poppin!)[20] I am proposing that reflecting on our purchases gives us an opportunity to investigate whether we are in alignment with our own unapologetic truth. Are we being manipulated by capitalism and the Body-Shame Profit Complex? If so, how we can take our power back?

> ### Radical Reflection
> *Our relationship with our money often mirrors our relationships with our bodies. When my relationship with me moves from a fear-based, lack-based, deficit-based relationship into a courageous, abundant, radical self-love relationship, intimate possibilities, financial possibilities, and creative possibilities unfold. Every single time!*

---

### Unapologetic Inquiry #14

*When was the last time you made a purchase because you didn't feel "good enough"? Did the purchase change how you felt? If so, how and for how long?*

## Best-Interest vs. Detriment Buying

Divesting from the Body-Shame Profit Complex requires us to imagine what a radical self-love economy might look like. Manifesting such an economy entails observing our personal impact in the worldwide marketplace and asking ourselves, "What kind of consumer am I?" I propose that most of our purchases generally fall into two primary categories: best-interest buying and detriment buying. Best-interest buying is a model that asks us to allow our economic investments, whether they be lattes, lipsticks, neckties, or stock portfolios, to reflect our commitment to radical self-love for our own lives and for the lives of others. Best-interest buying furthers our radical self-love journey by connecting how we spend our resources with what we truly want for our lives, not simply in the short term to avoid feelings of not being "enough." In this model, we ask ourselves if what we are buying is a desire rooted in radical self-love. Being a best-interest buyer does not happen overnight, and is not a zero-sum proposition. Given how rarely we are in control of how products are sourced and made, it is easy to make purchases that pass muster in regard to our personal motives for buying them while subsequently being a source of harm because of exploitative or unethical practices at the hands of the product makers. These systems of oppression are intricately woven together and will be hard to fully divest from. When we are unable to do no harm, our work is to do as little harm as possible. We do not become best-interest buyers by being judgmental jerks toward ourselves about our purchases or flagellating ourselves for being suckers conned by the BSPC. Instead we continue gently asking ourselves about our motives, intentions, and impact. Radical self-love calls us toward a deeper investigation: "Why am I compelled to spend $180 on wrinkle-defying serum?" Posing that question to ourselves is likely a more effective and loving strategy than haranguing ourselves for making said purchase. The act of inquiry serves as a lighthouse on our journey, there to help us locate our position in the wild seas of media and BSPC manipulation.

This does not mean we should be full-stop averse to changing our bodies, or that making makeup, fashion, or aesthetic choices is antithetical to radical self-love. What each of us needs to live in the fullness of our personal expression will be as varied as our individual bodies and dependent on our lived experiences. For example, when I have asked transgender people what they would do with $15,000, many have said they would spend it on gender-affirmation surgery (surgical procedures that change one's body to conform to one's gender identity).[21] This answer is unsurprising and completely aligned with radical self-love, which is about abiding in our most authentic selves. As we seek to do this, we are guided to move toward the most honest representation of our being. For some of us, moving away from body hyper-consciousness is key to that journey. For others, whose identities and bodies are more profoundly policed and erased by society, the desire to have those identities seen and affirmed is an essential aspect of the radical self-love journey. *Of course* we can wear makeup, join a gym, and color our hair. I am a loud proponent of being unapologetically adorned. But the practice of inquiry shows us where we have adopted the media indoctrination that connects our worth and value to our appearance and external selves. That is what I call detriment buying.

We know we are on the island of detriment buying when our honest inquiries about why we made a purchase show us that our motivations were more closely connected to our beliefs that we are

> **Radical Reflection**
> *Although our actions are important, we learn more about ourselves when we examine our motives. Radical self-love inquiry is less about judging ourselves for "what" we do and far more about compassionately asking ourselves "why?"*

somehow deficient or unworthy. Detriment buying leaves us feeling numbed out and disconnected from our bodies and our world. A great way to distinguish detriment buying from best-interest buying is to ask yourself, "Do I truly know I am no less worthy without these purchases? Am I buying this because it is an addition to the fullness of my already divine existence? Or is this purchase an effort to fix some presumed flaw? And if I think I am flawed, where is that message coming from? Who told me? Why do I believe them?" Our answers to these simple questions are a portal into a new way of being in relationship with ourselves, our bodies, and our money. Of course, this is not new at all; it is just our return to radical self-love!

## Unapologetic Inquiry #15

*Best-interest buying is also about reducing the harm our purchases cause other bodies. What are three ways you can reduce the harmful or exploitative outcomes of your purchases?*

## A Government for, by, and about Bodies

We cannot talk about bodies without talking about the systems that govern our bodies. If you are reading this book, you are probably located in some society with a government. That is, of course, unless you somehow found a copy of this book in a dark cave in a secret land where only you live, in which case ignore this section and consider yourself very lucky! The rest of us live under systems of government that are, by their very nature, about rules, laws, and bodies. Allocation of resources, attribution of rights, and assignment of responsibilities in a society are all functions of governance, and they impact the daily lives of the governed (all of whom just happen to be people with bodies). Our systems and structures do not exist in a vacuum. These systems in many ways mirror the societies that made

them. They are created and upheld by humans who have the same in-
doctrinations, beliefs, and shames that we all have. Those who govern
are not immune to the inheritance of body shame, either as recipients
or perpetrators. Our leaders mold and uphold systems of government
that directly affect our experiences of body shame and body-based
oppression. Officials regularly use these positions of power to codify
beliefs that are already present in their lives, in the lives of their con-
stituents, and in society at large. The power to create laws also endows
governments with the power to in-
fluence which bodies we accept as
"normal" and which we do not, all
through the validation of legality.
To varying degrees and without
very much thought, many of us
have accepted what we have been
told about our bodies and the bodies of others based on what our
government allows, sanctions, ignores, or criminalizes. As governments wield authority and oversee systems, they are in a unique posi-
tion to shape how we validate and stratify different bodies. Ultimately,
they are responsible for creating laws and entities that either protect
bodies or oppress them. Unfortunately, the history of government using its vast influence to ensure that all bodies are treated equitably has
been about as consistent as a game of Russian roulette.

> **Radical Reflection**
>
> *Systems of oppression stand or fall based on whether humans uphold or resist them. "We the people" have the power to uphold or resist body-based oppression.*

Did you know the following?

- Seventy-six countries have laws criminalizing homosexuality.
  In at least five countries, the death penalty can be applied to
  those found to be gay.[22]
- Immigrants can be deported from New Zealand for having a
  BMI (body mass index) over 35.[23]

- In Saudi Arabia, a fatwa (Islamic ruling) states that women should not drive because doing so could lead to the removal of the hijab, interactions with men, and "taboo" acts.[24]
- The "Asexualization Act" of 1909 made it legal in California to forcibly sterilize anyone the state deemed "mentally ill," "mentally deficient," or possessing a "feeblemindedness." California was still forcibly sterilizing female prison inmates as recently as 2010. Most were inmates of color.[25]
- In Malta, if a kidnapper, "after abducting a person, shall marry such person, he shall not be liable to prosecution."[26]
- In Greece, a 2012 measure allows police to "detain people suspected of being HIV positive and force them to be tested." The measure also urges landlords to evict tenants who are HIV positive (to counter a perceived "public health threat").[27]

Legislating body shame is not a draconian practice of centuries bygone. The above laws are modern-day examples of how our governments build body-based oppression into everyday lives, codifying inequity and injustice for all types of bodies. From LGBTQIA bodies, to fat bodies, to women's bodies, we live under systems that force us to judge, devalue, and discriminate against the bodies of others. Why, you might wonder, have we been so committed to discriminating against various bodies? To answer this question, we must look at the central currency of government: power.

The Center for American Women and Politics reports that thirty-six women have held a U.S. governorship since the first woman was elected as a governor in 1925.[28] By contrast, the United States has had over twenty-three hundred male governors in its history.[29] Globally, women hold only 23 percent of the total available seats in national parliaments.[30] Consider that women represent approximately half the human population, and it becomes glaringly clear that this disparity is the manifestation of gender inequity. Right now, your favorite men's rights activist is yelling, "These feminists are so dumb! Duh, there are fewer women because women just don't get involved in politics as much as men do." My contemplative reply might be, "Hmm . . . I wonder how much the 144 years American women went without voting rights impacted that?" Even today in many countries, women must battle laws forbidding or obstructing their involvement in government. Even without the presence of such laws, women's involvement in the political landscape cannot be separated from the scrutiny, objectification, and sexism they still face while running for office. All over the world women must traverse a hostile terrain that questions female suitability for political service while excusing gender discrimination by using outdated, disparaging tropes about female intelligence, ability, and acumen as justification for that bias. Naomi Wolfe, journalist and author of *The Beauty Myth,* writes, "A culture fixated on female thinness is not an obsession about female beauty but an obsession about female obedience. Dieting is the most potent political sedative in history. A quietly mad population is a tractable one."[31]

Wolfe strategically illustrates how body-shame social messaging is used as a means of controlling and centralizing political power. We need look no further than the 2016 U.S. presidential election to see Wolfe's thesis in action. Candidate Hillary Clinton was exhaustingly scrutinized about her aesthetic presentation. Outfits, makeup, hairstyles were all fodder for the twenty-four-hour news cycle. Even the pro-Hillary, hundred-thousand-plus-member Facebook group Pantsuit Nation chose her penchant for eschewing skirts and dresses as the name of their collective, inadvertently directing public focus to her physical appearance rather than her decades of political experience.

At every corner, women's political access hinges on society's ability to see them in alignment with the default ideals of women first and then politicians. But political gatekeeping based on bodies exists beyond the realm of sex and gender binaries. In workshops, I often ask participants to consider the thirty-six women who have been governors throughout the country's history and to take guesses at what those numbers might be if we were to break them down by various identities. How many people of color have been governor? What about the number of openly gay or lesbian people? How about people with disabilities? Or transgender folks? Undoubtedly people begin to see how those numbers winnow down to fewer and fewer diverse bodies being represented in our "representative" government. But we do not have to guess. The numbers speak for themselves:

- Twenty-four governors have been people of color.[32]
- Six governors have been disabled.[33]
- Two governors have been openly gay or lesbian.[34]
- Zero have been openly transgender.

Remember, most us live at the intersection of gender, age, race, disability, etc., our identities overlapping. Which means representation is nearly nonexistent for bodies living at the axis of multiple identities. The United States has had only one woman of color serve as governor and one lesbian woman. All the other intersections of identity . . . zero. This country is not an anomaly in its history of centralizing political power toward a very specific sort of body; most nations have a default body in their government structures. Although social and cultural realities may shift what those bodies look like, using default bodies to establish a social hierarchy and distribute power and resources is a global phenomenon. The statistics above illustrate an irrefutable truth: body shame and oppression are both symptoms of and tools in a far more complex and sweeping system of access and resources. A system that impacts not only how we feel about ourselves but also our opportunities and ability to thrive in the world. There is a reason we hate our bodies, and it isn't because of Curtis, our mamas, or even our low self-esteem. We are saddled with body shame because it is an age-old system whose roots and pockets are deep. Body shame flourishes in our world because profit and power depend on it.

## Unapologetic Inquiry #16

*How does body shame impact political power? How has body shame made you less powerful?*

## Call It What It Is: Body Terrorism

At the beginning of the book I described how the containers of self-esteem and self-confidence simply cannot hold the breadth and depth of radical self-love. As humans, we're in need of a radical love to transform how our world deals with bodies. I hope by this point in the book I've made my case. Our work must be radical if we are to combat the consistent inundation of toxic media messages, laws, and regulations seeping body shame and body-based oppression into every aspect of our society. Inequity in our government systems, manipulation in our media—no matter the structure under examination, ultimately each of us bears the personal, social, and political burden of a widespread and deeply troubling relationship with bodies. The results of this reality are nothing short of devastating. Gross inequality and disenfranchisement across social experiences, poor public-health outcomes, and unjust legislation are systemic representations of centuries of infusing body shame into every sector of public and private life. A National Center for Health Statistics report (as recounted in the *New York Times*) indicated that suicide rates in 2014 were the highest they had been in thirty years. American Indians, a community whose bodies have been met with an interminable history of oppression, erasure, and inequity, saw the highest rise in rates, with a horrifying increase of 89 percent.[35] A ProPublica analysis of federal data regarding police-involved shootings found that young Black men between ages fifteen and nineteen were twenty-one times more likely to be killed by the police than young White men of the same age.[36] By the first half of 2017 the Human Rights Campaign had tracked the rise of over 115 pieces of new anti-LGBT legislation across the United States.[37] These numbers tell a story about how our societies fare under the pressures of body-based oppressions.

Entire communities are dying from epidemic levels of suicide. Parents around the country are immobilized with the fear that a routine traffic stop might result in the indiscriminate murder of their child at the hands of a police officer. (This fear is so commonplace that thousands of Black parents find themselves having "the talk" with their kids: a detailed discussion of what their children should

### Radical Reflection

*Our beliefs about bodies disproportionately impact those whose race, gender, sexual orientation, ability, and age deviate from our default notions. The further from the default, the greater the impact. We are all affected—but not equally.*

do if the police stop them, in the hope that they might prepare them with enough information to arrive home safe each night.) No sooner than gay and lesbian people celebrate the landmark legislative win of being able to legally marry the person they love, they are forced to watch state after state sanction their continued discrimination in restaurants, in medical facilities, and on the job. Our world is disconnected from the site of these inequities. We look at statistics and see policy and laws, forgetting how they are created by and enacted on our bodies. Across gender, sexual orientation, race, size, age, and ability level, our systems are constantly affirming or denouncing bodies, communicating to us what we should and should not consider valid about other people's bodies while simultaneously detailing for us what we should and should not accept about our own.

On December 28, 2014, seventeen-year-old trans youth Leelah Alcorn intentionally stepped into highway traffic and was hit by an eighteen-wheeled truck. In her suicide note, Leelah detailed her family's rejection of her trans identity and their refusal to give her permission to receive gender-affirming surgery.[38] It is tempting to see Leelah's story as the individual allegory of a highly religious family's dogma and its tragic impact on a teen. But to allow the analysis to stop there would be to miss the myriad ways in which systems much bigger than Leelah's family failed to protect her. Leelah's story indicts our entire society for its unwillingness to care for all bodies, thus making it virtually impossible for some of us to live lives of radical self-love—or even to continue wanting to live at all. A lack of school-based resources able to address the needs of trans students, inaccessible mental health supports, a society that demands that bodies conform to rigid gender assignments: these larger systemic realities contributed as much to Leelah's heart-rending death as her family's bigotries. A long line of people and systems blocked Leelah's vision of a rich and authentic future for herself. That obstruction ended in her death.

### Unapologetic Inquiry #17

*If you could share something with Leelah that would have given her hope, what would you have said? Write it down. Share it with yourself on the days you are struggling to find hope.*

Living with mounting evidence that society at every turn will reject our attempts to exist unapologetically in our bodies is to live in a

state of terror. Dragging ourselves through a lifetime of self-hate en-
dorsed and encouraged by our media and our political and economic systems is a terrifying way to live, and yet millions of people
exist in this constant state of fear every day. It is an act of terrorism
against our bodies to perpetuate body shame and to support body-
based oppression. I call this "body terrorism."

    *Terrorism* is defined as "the systematic use of terror especially as a
means of coercion."[39] It takes no more than a brief review of the his-
toric and present-day examples of media manipulation and legislative oppression to acknowledge that we are indeed being coerced
into body shame for both economic and political reasons. When using
the term *body terrorism,* I have been met with resistance and accused
of hyperbole. "You are being dismissive of the danger of 'real' terrorism," detractors have said. This knee-jerk response to our understanding of terrorism is shaped by a public discourse that continues
to separate the fear and violence we navigate every day in our bodies
from the more overtly political violence we see happening around
the world. We must not minimize or negate the impact of being told
to hate or fear our bodies and the bodies of others. Living in a society structured to profit from our self-hate creates a dynamic in which
we are so terrified of being ourselves that we adopt terror-based
ways of being in our bodies. All this is fueled by a system that makes
large quantities of money off our shame and bias. These experiences
are not divergent but complementary.

    On the morning of the presidential inauguration of Donald Trump
I was leaving Washington, DC, after hosting an event called the Peace
Ball the night before. When I arrived at the airport and proceeded
through the body scanner, I was stopped for additional screening.
Apparently, my groin area had signaled the machine's alert system,
and I was going to be subjected to a pat down. This was not my first
time navigating TSA screening procedures. I am, after all, a fat Black
woman with the word *radical* in her job title on her business cards.

The TSA agent rubbed her hands up my inner thigh and without warning rubbed my vulva. My response was involuntary. "Why are you touching my vagina?" I blurted out loud enough for the entire security line to hear. Confounded by my outburst, the TSA agent quickly called for her supervisor, who demanded that I be taken to a private screening room where I would be less disruptive as the agents groped my genitalia. Powerless, I wept silently as the agent completed the pat down, and then I exited the private room, shaken by a deep sense of violation. I had been sexually assaulted—simply in order to be able carry on to my next destination, under the orders of the government, and paid for by my tax dollars.

The next day, anxiety hijacked me as I walked into a different airport while headed home from my travels. Initially I couldn't locate the source of the anxiety buzzing through my chest and legs, and then I recalled the events of the day before: I was having a trauma response. My body had catalogued yesterday's incident as a traumatic violation and was bracing in terror for the experience to happen again. Later, I learned from several transgender friends that the TSA scanners are designed to alert agents to "anomalies" in the groin area. Specifically, agents are instructed to additionally screen all people whose groins appear to differ from their perceived gender. Across the country, large numbers of transgender people are also being forced to navigate similar invasive sexual traumas simply to board a plane. We are told that the procedures of the Transportation Security Administration are supposed to make us safer. I did not feel safe. I was terrified and without recourse. While I stood in the "private screening room" with tears rolling down my face, the least of my concerns was some random person living out a political vendetta against the United States during my flight. I was terrified of having my genitalia touched without my consent by a stranger as a requisite for passage to my next destination. This is body terrorism. Believing that it is preferable to walk into the path of an eighteen-wheeler than to live another day being rejected by the whole of society is a belief rooted firmly in the soil of being subjected to body terrorism.

---

### Unapologetic Inquiry #18

*Can you recall an incident when you felt a sense of terror about being in your body? What did you do to navigate the feeling?*

---

The historical and contemporary violence associated with body hatred is widespread and horrific. We cannot continue to normalize these actions as simply inconvenient or unfortunate. The outcomes of body terrorism are deadly. From violence against people of color (e.g., lynching, slavery, the Holocaust, internment camps); to LGBTQIA bodies being regularly assaulted, murdered, and driven to suicide; to rape and sexual assault; to the bombing of abortion clinics and the murder of physicians based on women's rights to autonomy over their own bodies; to the involuntary sterilization of people with disabilities; to the debilitating shame that people around the world live with as a result of the psychological attacks our social and media machines wage against us (ending in bulimia, anorexia, addiction, stigma, racism, homophobia, ableism, sizeism, ageism, transphobia, mass self-hatred, and senseless violence)—it is clear that there is nothing rhetorical or hyperbolic about detailing the impacts of body hatred and calling the promotion of such hatred on any scale an act of body-based terrorism.[40]

The framework of radical self-love seeks to engage people in the process of individual transformation. But as importantly it seeks to dismantle the structural and systemic emotional, psychological, and physical violence meted out against "different" bodies all over the planet. It serves those who profit from our self-hatred to minimize its impact and disconnect it from the larger social framework of violence and intimidation that allows oppression and injustice to thrive. Discrimination, social inequality, and injustice are manifestations of our inability to make peace with the body: our own and others'. By making these connections we build the foundation to foster a world of radical, unapologetic self-love, which translates to radical human action in the service of a more just and compassionate world.

**Radical Reflection**

*Take a moment to consider how body terrorism has impacted your life and the lives of people you love. Imagine what might be possible in a world without it.*

# 3

# Building a Radical
# Self-Love Practice in
# an Age of Loathing

## Mapping Our Way out of Shame and into
## Radical Self-Love

Recall from Chapter 1 my discussion of the Three Peaces, which we must reckon with if we want to abandon the body-shame army and commence our radical self-love assignment. To recap, kicking body shame in the butt means we must be willing to do the following:

1. Make peace with not understanding.
2. Make peace with difference.
3. Make peace with our bodies.

Well, my friend, we have arrived on the shores of the final P. Up to this point, we have unpacked the difference between self-confidence and radical self-love. We have learned why self-love must be a radical act if we want a transformed world. We've revisited the ick and discomfort of our body-shame origins, disrobed the media and the Body-Shame Profit Complex, explored the role of government in shaping rights and laws that privilege some bodies while punishing others. We have examined the traumatizing and fatal outcomes of living under a system of body terrorism. If you are currently considering a permanent relocation to that autonomous cave without a government that I mentioned earlier, I want you to know that I do not blame you. Radical self-love can feel like an impossibility when observed beside the deluge of body shame we see falling all around us. What I also want you to know is that *radical self-love is not an impossibility*. It is not even a destination. *It is your inherent sense of self.* You came here, to this planet, as unapologetic radical love. Body terrorism depends on your amnesia for its survival. Our singular focus in this chapter is to help you practice the third Peace. Making peace with your body is not about finding some obscure pathway to the peninsula of "liking my thighs." Making peace with your body is about awakening to who you have always been: the physical, spiritual, and energetic manifestation of radical self-love. Together, we will disrupt decades of tired body-shame practices using the only map we ever needed for this journey: a map back to ourselves.

Body terrorism is a hideous tower whose primary support beam is the belief that there is a hierarchy of bodies. We uphold the system by internalizing this hierarchy and using it to situate our own value and worth in the world. When our personal value is dependent on the lesser value of other bodies, radical self-love is unachievable.

By this point, my hope is that you can see how you and millions of others have been manipulated into a system of body shame. More importantly, I want you to know that this system is destructible, and the fastest way to obliterate its control over us is to do the

> **Radical Reflection**
> *Theodore Roosevelt is famously quoted as saying, "Comparison is the thief of Joy." He was totally right! Go get your joy back!*

scary work of tearing down those pillars of hierarchy inside ourselves. At the same time, we must trust that what will be left standing is our own divine enoughness, absent of any need for comparison. *Living a radical self-love life is a process of de-indoctrination.* It demands that we look unflinchingly at our current set of beliefs about ourselves and the world and get willing to explore them. I call this the act of being fear-facing. Fear-facingness is not the absence of fear but the interrogation of it. While agonizing over the completion of this book, I spent some time emptying my brain at a friend's home on a private beach in Long Island, Bahamas. The island was slow and kind, like a good grandfather. During one of our excursions we drove westward, down miles of crumbled, unforgiving asphalt, until we arrived at a small beach. The sign at the edge of the road read, "Warning. Dean's Hole is the deepest in the world. Swim at Your Own Risk." Two feet from the beach shore the cerulean water stops being waist high, and within a few steps the ocean floor drops into a cavernous 663-feet-deep hole. Despite my being a competent swimmer, fear consumed me. I was certain that the mouth of the deep blue hole would suck me down to its watery floor. In my research, I would later discover that my fear mirrored the exact superstitions that keep native islanders away from the hole. Needless to say, I kept my distance.

It was at Dean's Hole where I met Davide Carrera, a free-diving champion from Italy. Free diving entails using a cable to descend into extreme ocean depths without the use of breathing equipment. Davide holds his country's record with a 111-meter dive (yes, that is the equivalent of diving off a thirty-five-story building)![1] He was taking a break from competition and enjoying the beach with his fellow divers when we struck up a conversation. (It is in these chance encounters that I am reminded that if we are open to it, we will find confirmation of our divine pathway all around us.) "The dive is a spiritual thing," Davide said. "I learn how to listen to my body. I must listen or I will die. In the water, I must learn the difference between fear and danger." He did not know it, but Davide was describing the journey of radical self-love. It is damn scary to probe the depths of the thoughts, ideas, and subconscious principles governing our daily lives. To be fear-facing is to learn the distinction between fear and danger. It is to look directly at the source of the fear and assess if we are truly in peril or if we are simply afraid of the unknown. The unknown is like fog, and, of course, fog is frightening. Who knows what obstructions could be lurking about? What if there is a deer soon to be splayed on my windshield? What if I careen off a cliff while driving in the thick soup of fog? Living with body shame and body terrorism is to be stuck in an endless "what if" fog: a place of inertia. The only way out of the fog is through it. We must dive into the unknown, trusting that our bodies will help us discern fear from danger. There is always a clearing on the other side of the fog. To be fear-facing is to navigate cautiously and with alertness but to continue our journey. Before we parted, I asked Davide what continues to call him to the sport of free diving. He beamed at me, the Bahamian sun lucent behind him, and said, "Every meter is a tiny freedom." Yes, it is. So, let's dive in!

---

### Unapologetic Inquiry #19

*Ask yourself, "In what ways has the fog of living in body shame hindered my most amazing life? What is incomplete, unexplored, ignored inside me because of my belief that something about me and my body is wrong?"*

---

## Thinking, Being, Doing

You can't self-help your way back to radical self-love. Reading this book will not be enough to get you there because radical self-love is a return to the love of our whole being. It requires a whole-being approach to our lives and bodies. Living a radical self-love life is a process of:

- thinking
- doing
- being

Have you ever spent time with your thoughts? Whew, talk about a scene from the film *The Exorcist*. Our thoughts are an amalgamation of all manner of input mixed with a dash of original content. Often it's a mess in there, a vessel filled with self-loathing and judgment. It's unsurprising that we avoid being present with our thoughts. We think tons of repugnant, petrifying, miserable things about our own bodies and other folks' bodies every single day. It's easy to slip into a pit of shame for having these thoughts. Unfortunately, the sense of shame keeps us distant and detached from our personal center of governance. It puts us out of operational control. Have you ever felt like you were living your life on autopilot? Somehow you just keep recycling old behaviors and ideas that you know do not serve you, but you can't seem to interrupt them. Yeah (in my best Michael Jackson vocal impersonation), you are not alone! That sense of autopilot is the result of being disconnected from our thoughts. Without our awareness, thoughts run covert operations all through our lives, assassinating our sense of worth and blowing up our connections with other humans. When we avoid our thoughts, they go rogue. Awareness of our thoughts highlights the how and why of our behaviors. It gives us a fighting chance at transforming how we live in the world.

"But how do I break out of the fear of exploring the catacombs of my thoughts?" Great question! Survey says, remember, *You are not your thoughts!* Our thoughts are a hybrid of information forged from our own experiences, traumas, successes, failures, etc., and massive input from our external world. All those media messages about "good" bodies and "normal" bodies: they're in your thoughts. All the government-endorsed ideas of safe bodies and dangerous bodies: they're in your thoughts. You have been given thoughts, and just like that shame sweater you do not have to keep them.

On a flight to Morocco several years ago, I was convinced that the all-Arab, all-male flight-attendant crew were terrorists preparing to hijack the plane. What a horrible thought! I felt awful for the judgments and irrational fear I was having about these men based on their bodies. But the truth is I didn't give myself those thoughts. A 2012 article on the website of the Society of Personality and Social Psychology reviewed multiple studies and found that "people exposed to 'Arabs-as-terrorists' media may be more likely to perceive a seemingly neutral interaction with an Arab as threatening or aggressive, thereby influencing the course of the interaction."[2] Constant visual images of Arab men hijacking planes and buses and kidnapping Americans had been poured into my psyche for almost twenty years. Consciously, I knew that those images I saw on television were not a representation of all Arab men. I knew that the U.S. "war on terror" was causing grave harm to Arab and Muslim people around the world. It did not matter that the statistical likelihood of my plane being hijacked by twelve very attractive, uniformed flight attendants was beyond negligible. Per a Cato Institute analysis, my chances of dying in an attack committed by a foreign-born terrorist were 1 in 3.6 million, also known as, not very likely.[3]

Despite all my information, the thoughts were still there. But because I have practiced being aware of my thoughts, I could identify how the thoughts were mine—as in, happening inside my brain—but they were not me. They were part of a bounty of ideas

> ## Radical Reflection
> *Say it again, for the folks in the bleachers:* You are not your thoughts! *That said, avoiding your thoughts will not help you train your brain to think new ones.* You must look at them with gentle kindness and say, "Thank you for sharing." And with love, release them.

and messages I had received from multiple sources that had sub-consciously penetrated my psyche. My ability to notice the thoughts and distinguish them from my own authentic ideas helped me source where they were coming from. Those thoughts were not me, and I had a choice about whether to act on them or not.

---

### Unapologetic Inquiry #20

*Can you recall a time when you had a body-shaming thought about someone else's body? Can you identify where some of those ideas came from?*

---

Being intimately connected to our thoughts is not enough to change our behaviors. Knowing why we do something will not necessarily keep us from doing it. Doing is a choice. It is an act of will. Doing often demands that we act despite our thoughts. When we are no longer on autopilot, we are forced to deal with the discomfort of new action. Think of radical self-love as resistance training against our decades-old, tight, calcified thoughts. Adopting actions that promote radical self-love is comparable to working a muscle that has not been moved in years. It's going to be sore and tender. You are going to be tired. But the exhaustion and frustration will lessen over time, and there will be ease where there once was pain. Old habits of body-shaming yourself, judging the bodies of others under your breath, acting from a sense of failure or lack of self-worth will become uncomfortable behaviors, and radical self-love action will begin to feel like the path of least resistance. Over time, you will notice that your thoughts flow in alignment with your behaviors. The junk in your brain will start to occupy less space, and when it starts to reclutter your thoughts you will recognize it and move it out. You are thinking and acting in radical self-love.

Have you ever met someone and thought, "Wow, Mary just ema-nates love from her whole being"? The experience of being around someone who radiates a discernable energy is an act of being. Though it is not always a positive experience. We engage every day with people whose energy is not welcoming—sometimes even downright hostile—but we also meet people who radiate unencumbered love. Children are a glorious example of this ability to radiate love. Having not yet experienced layers of body shame, young kids are reflections of the source relationship of all our beings: love.

> **Radical Reflection**
>
> *Notice the next time your actions are not in alignment with your thoughts. The discomfort you feel is trying to tell you something. It is pushing you beyond just thinking or doing, toward radical self-love being.*

We, too, can access that source relationship. Through the power of thought and action we become who we have always been; we enter a new way of being in our bodies and in the world. We return to our inherent state of being: radical self-love.

## Four Pillars of Practice

We know that adopting a radical self-love lifestyle is a process of thinking, doing, and being. But changing the way we think, act, and are in our daily lives can feel like an assignment of planetary proportions. Implementing practices to structure this endeavor is the equivalent of turning on the high beams amid the fog. Rather than collapsing under an avalanche of new ideas and behaviors, we can install signposts and guardrails that help us know if we are still on the road to radical self-love. The four pillars of practice can help us corral our wily thinking, fortify love-laden action, and give us access to a new way of being in the world. The pillars are:

- Taking out the Toxic
- Mind Matters

- Unapologetic Action
- Collective Compassion

Dismantling body shame and body terrorism is a process of de-indoctrination requiring that we excavate the thoughts we have internalized about bodies and evict the voices of judgment, hierarchy, and shame. Remember when I recounted how my fear of sharing a selfie was an early prompt in my radical self-love journey? The voice I heard in my head telling me I was too fat, ugly, and black to post the photo was not my voice. It was the propaganda of body shame, the "outside voice." Our inherent sense of radical self-love doesn't speak to us with cruelty or viciousness. Radical self-love does not malign our gender, sexuality, race, disability, weight, age, acne, scars, illnesses. A world of body terrorism that impugns us because of our identities is the only thing that would dare speak to us with such malice. Just as the Three Peaces offer us a framework for divesting from a lifetime of shame and judgment, the four pillars teach us to make peace with our bodies by distinguishing and diminishing the outside voice and cultivating a practice of listening more deeply to our authentic selves, our radical self-love voice, our "inside voice."

The first two pillars, taking out the toxic and mind matters, ask us to imagine the inside and outside voices as though they were volume knobs in our minds. These radical self-love practices teach us how to adjust the sound and filter the static, turning up our authentic voice

> ### Radical Reflection
> I have always had a very loud voice. My mother would constantly admonish me for talking too loudly. "Use your inside voice!" she would say. Next time you hear someone speaking body shame over themselves, politely suggest that they use their "inside voice," and share what the phrase means.

and tuning out our body-shame brainwashing. The pillar unapologetic action integrates our thinking with our physical selves, moving our radical self-love practice out of our heads and into our bodies. Lastly, the pillar of collective compassion synthesizes how we emanate radical self-love, learning to radiate love through our own beings and onto the beings of others. At the end of the book you will find a Radical Self-Love Toolkit. It offers concrete action steps designed to help you move through the thinking, doing, being process, ultimately landing you in the seat of your most powerful location: reconnected to your inherent sense of radical self-love.

## Pillar 1: Taking Out the Toxic

To live in a world of body terrorism is akin to forcibly imbibing three 7-Eleven Big Gulps of body shame daily. From the moment we turn on a television, radio, or computer in the morning until we close the laptop or put the phone on silent at night, we are inundated with messages relaying our supposed inherent deficiency. The average adult consumes fifteen and a half hours of media each day, and even when they don't contain overt body shame, the shows we watch, the music we listen to, and the articles we read deliver messages about bodies in the world, including our own.[4] Taking in toxic messages blocks our pathway to radical self-love without any real effort on our part. Just walking down the street or standing in the grocery store checkout line can be a stroll down body-shame lane thanks to billboards, bus advertisements, and tabloid covers. By engaging in the everyday activities of our society, we subconsciously absorb views about our bodies that are antithetical to radical self-love. Therefore, being connected to our thoughts is a crucial process for battling body shame.

Marketers diversify their body-terrorism tactics with both conscious and subconscious directives. There is nothing subconscious about "Don't delay! Lose that unsightly belly fat now!" Advertisements like this are designed for immediacy, urging you to act now because your body is awful!

---

### Unapologetic Inquiry #21

*What was your last body-shame impulse purchase? Can you recall what thoughts moved you to make the purchase?*

---

Equally sinister are the advertisements that remind us by repetition and erasure that unless we are youthful, blonde, thin, able-bodied, and muscular, with perfectly white teeth and glossy hair, we are fatally flawed and will need their product . . . eventually. (By the way, *no one* is all those things forever.) Advertisers and product makers want your money now. Are they willing to wait until you have watched sixty hours of television actors with perfect ivory teeth and have finally awakened to the epiphany that you must buy teeth-whitening strips? Of course! But why bother waiting? Body-Shame Profit Complex profiteers know it is easier and more economically efficient to sell us body shame directly, to simply say "You suck" rather than allude to it. They prefer to highlight your epic flaws in grand detail on repeat until you get up off your couch and go give them your money!

Not only does this toxic messaging impact our spending, turning us into detriment buyers, but it also impacts how we talk about ourselves and others. Let's say you are out shopping for new jeans, and as you begin to try them on you think aloud, "I have to get rid of this unsightly belly flab!" You know you have never used the words *unsightly* and *flab* together, but suddenly you are a parrot for body-shame advertisers, speaking their carefully crafted messages over your own body. Toxic messages become our internal outside voice. After we've ingested enough body shame, these declarations become the narrative through which we speak about our own bodies, often without even noticing.

What can we do to get out of the toxic sludge of media marketing? Limit our media intake. If we cannot limit it, be intentional about what we ingest. Next time you are watching television, notice what commercials your favorite shows air between scenes. Those commercials indicate what advertisers believe about you as a consumer. Commercials use racial and gender stereotypes to target your wallets because they know that doing so works. This is a perfect place to put best-interest buying into practice. Television shows make money through ratings and advertising. Each show you watch puts money in some producer's and advertiser's pockets. Ask yourself, "Does this show and its commercials align with my radical self-love values?" If the answer is no, then the next question is "Why am I giving them my money?" If we think of our time and brain capacity as dollars, we may become a bit more particular about how we spend them. When we are connected to our thoughts, we can identify how they are being dragged along by toxic media. If you have a body-shame hangover after you watch, read, or listen to something, it might be time to take out the toxic. Tools 1 and 2 listed in Chapter 5 offer concrete ways you can minimize toxic body shame in your daily life.

## Pillar 2: Mind Matters

If pillar 1 is the equivalent of a body-shame yard sale (except we don't want anyone else to buy this junk), then pillar 2 is emptying out the attic and basement and considering what we might do with all the amazing space we've freed up. Once we have stopped imbibing body shame on a daily basis, we can begin to explore how our old ways of thinking have kept us stuck in cycles that dishonor our bodies. Body shame not only shapes how we see our bodies; it also clouds the lens through which we view our lives. If living a radical self-love life is a process of thinking, doing, and being, then "mind matters" asks us to try on some new mental attire. Let's call it the season's latest collection on the radical self-love runway.

Over the years, we have collected some crappy beliefs about our bodies. We've been taught that our bodies are entities to control and subjugate. We have treated our bodies like machines that are always on the fritz. In Eve Ensler's 2011 TED Talk, "Suddenly My Body," she details how she spent most of her life disembodied, never considering her body a part of her being.[5] This remained true until she wrote *The Vagina Monologues* during a period in which she describes herself as becoming a "driven vagina." Still, her body was outside her. She saw it as a utensil, an instrument she used to get things done. It was when she got cancer that she realized her body was not an implement at her disposal but a part of her. Her body did not have cancer; she had cancer. Eve discovered that she and her body would have to integrate if she wanted to fight the disease that had attacked them both. They needed each other. The concept of "mind matters" asks us to reconsider our relationship with our bodies. How do we end the Cold War with it and become allies in achieving our best lives? This pillar of practice is about reconciliation. In her poem "Three," Nayyirah Waheed captures the fullness of the second pillar in five perfect lines: "and i said to my body. softly. / 'i want to be your friend.' / it took a long breath. / and replied / 'i have been waiting my / whole life for this.' "[6]

*Guess what? Your brain is part of your body!* Why am I yelling this? Because too often we treat our brain as though it's a separate operating system tucked away in a room we call the skull. Our tendency to divorce our brains from our bodies is one of the sneaky ways in which body shame thrives. Isolating our brains gives us permission to treat them differently. Depression, bipolar disorder, and other examples of neurodivergence[7] are stigmatized because we are unwilling to extend the same care and treatment to our brains that we afford our bodies. If I broke my arm and never went to a see a doctor, not only would I be in extreme pain but the people in my life would be incensed by such a reckless choice. Yet we make statements like

"It's all in your head" all the time, minimizing the experiences of our brains and neglecting their care.

Reintegrating our brains and our bodies is a necessity for a radical self-love life. Pillar 2 highlights how our reintegration gives us access to new levels of care and offers us new opportunities to examine our thought patterns and, with hard work, create new ones. I may never get rid of my clinical depression, but I can disentangle

> **Radical Reflection**
> *Phrases like "Get over it!" and "It's all in your head" are rooted in ableism. They are body terrorism against non-normative brains. Let's stop telling people to "get over it" and start asking, "How can I help you heal?"*

it from body shame. Mind-matter tools like meditation and reframing have helped me see my depression as another unique way my body exists in the world rather than as a shame to avoid or hide.

Expanding our mind's capacity for radical self-love means we may need to tear down some mental walls. If radical self-love is an open floor plan, expanding our space for connection and joy, rigidity and judgment are concrete walls, cutting off visibility and partitioning us off from our best lives. Pillar 2 is about expansive thinking, and expansive thinking is not possible unless we see our bodies and our lives with nuance. We are not either/or beings; we comprise a multitude of grey shades. Inviting love into our contradictions and uncertainties takes a wrecking ball to those concrete slabs of separation, giving us much more space to decorate with love. Check out tools 3, 4, and 5 in Chapter 5 for powerful illustrations of how mind matters can create the mental spaciousness we need to practice radical self-love.

## Pillar 3: Unapologetic Action

If we are diligent in our practice of pillars 1 and 2, the volume of our external body shame can over time become a light buzz while our own resounding voice of radical self-love begins to ring loudly in our ears. There is no better time to get started on the "doing" portion of this work. Radical self-love is a muscle, and as with every other muscle, if we do not work it, atrophy will set in. Living in a world of body terrorism is like having our sense of value and innate worth set in a plaster cast for decades. Cracking open the cast and moving through the world in tune with our bodies can feel like working out our trapezius muscle. (What does that muscle even do?) There has never been a more perfect time to lean into the discomfort and fear. Remember, most of the fear is just fog.

It is difficult to deeply love a stranger. Familiarity breeds fondness. Pillar 3, unapologetic action, asks us to get to know these bodies of ours. If you have been avoiding looking at or touching your body, this is your chance to shift. By now, we understand our avoidance of being intimate with our bodies as part of being conditioned to believe that our bodies are bad, wrong, or disgusting. No one wants to hang out with a bad, wrong body. As we clear out those thoughts we are better able to see our bodies for what they truly are: amazing vessels, capable of awesome feelings, sensations, and experiences. By getting to know them, we open ourselves to deeper levels of pleasure, care, and ultimately radical love. Pillar 3 invites you to take yourself on a body expedition and discover your own remarkable landscape.

Not only have we avoided intimately knowing our bodies; we have forgotten that our bodies like doing stuff—walking, dancing, running, having sex! Body shame has severed our love of activity. In the chronicles of body shame, movement became a thing we avoided lest we jiggle while in motion! Unapologetic action is our departure from those old stories, prompting us to reconnect to the joys of movement. Many of us cannot recall a time when moving our bodies was something other than a way to punish them for failing to meet society's fictitious ideals. But just as we were once babies who loved our bodies, we were also babies who loved moving them. We can invite ourselves back to this place. There was magic there.

Pillar 3 is not singularly focused on our physical selves; it also summons us to new action by telling ourselves new stories. In Chapter 2 we discussed the characteristics of our early memories of body shame. We acknowledged how the things we were teased about or shamed for became part of how we saw ourselves later in life. Those early incidents became the yarn tethering our adult selves to our childhood histories of shame and isolation. Unapologetic action empowers us to make new stories, better than the ones we've been saddled with for years. Humans have made up stories since the beginning of time. Some of the stories have helped us understand this wild ride through humanity, whereas others have kept us cut off from radical self-love. We no longer must be bound by crappy stories. Humans made them up. You are human. Make a better story. Take unapologetic action on a regular basis with tools 6, 7, and 8 in Chapter 5.

## Pillar 4: Collective Compassion

In the beginning of my workshops, I tell participants that they can do everything I say, employ the Three Peaces in every area of their life, trace their body-shame origin story back to its inception, denounce the Body-Shame Profit Complex from the highest rooftop, and rock the first three pillars like nobody's business. But if they avoid pillar 4, collective compassion, then radical self-love will continue to elude them. Every word in this book is unsustainable without the fourth pillar. Collective compassion is the "being" part of radical self-love. It is our internal compass, quickly alerting us when we are off course. Not only does collective compassion provide an internal structure of governance (i.e., the rules that guide our personal work), it is also the bridge to the *socially* transformative power of radical self-love. Collective compassion offers direction for how we ought to treat ourselves, but as importantly, it is our directive for "being" with others.

Have you ever run into someone many years after the last time you saw them only to discover that they had undergone some phenomenal inner transformation? I am not talking about weight loss or a new haircut. I am talking a brand-new life. Perhaps they got sober after years of addiction. Maybe they healed a relationship that appeared completely irreparable from the outside. Whatever the transformation, when you saw them, you were flabbergasted. I am guessing your next thought was not, "Hey! I could totally do that!" For most humans, transformation does not seem achievable from the distant shores of another person's life. From far away, transformation looks like a miracle, or the result of magical powers possessed by the transformed person. Transformation is not magic. It's hard work. But it is also doable work. When we can see another person's labor toward their transformation, we know it is not some secret sauce but instead a daily commitment to a new way of life.

Up close we can also see that they are not doing the work alone! Transformation and healing demand that we open ourselves up to others. For many of us, this is the highest hurdle on the radical self-love road. Body shame and body terrorism have made us profoundly distrusting. We've been judged and mocked too many times. We have vowed to never subject ourselves to such hurt again. I want you to know I understand. But learning to trust others is indivisible from learning to trust yourself. You will need to practice both to get back to radical self-love. If you are working to rid yourself of years of body shame by being Clark Kent in a phone booth, I am sorry, love, but you will not come out as Superman. You are going to need someone to lean against while you pull up those tights. Truthfully, radical self-love is not the work of superheroes but of community and connection. Pillar 4 asks you to move beyond self-reliance to collective care. We must learn to *be* with each other if we plan to get free.

Before body shame stripped us of our inherent sense of self-worth, it stripped us of compassion. We saw failure in every mirror; we judged our every thought. We berated and abused ourselves because we were berated and abused by others. We thought the outside voice was our own, and we let it run roughshod over our lives. And then we judged ourselves for judging ourselves, trapped on a hamster wheel of self-flagellation. Oh, honey, that is no way to live. Without compassion for ourselves we will never stay on the road of radical self-love. Without compassion for others we can only replicate the world we have always known. Radical self-love is not about "getting it right." "Getting it right" is a body-shame paradigm. Radical self-love is honoring how we are all products of a rigged system designed to keep us stuck in stigma and shame. The only way to beat that system is by giving ourselves something the system never will: compassion.

The four pillars of practice will support our personal radical self-love journeys, offering light along the road and helping us correct course when needed. If you use them in conjunction with the tools outlined in Chapter 5, you will have much of what you need to build a daily thinking, doing, and being routine of radical self-love. I am totally jazzed for you . . . really! But our work together is not done. Now that we have done the work to transform our lives, it's time to take on the world!

# 4

# A New Way Ordered by Love

## A World for All Bodies Is a World for Our Bodies

Perhaps you have missed it thus far, but I have an agenda to which I am obnoxiously wedded. It's a simple agenda. I want to change the world by convincing you to love every facet of yourself, radically and unapologetically, even the parts you don't like. And through this work, illustrate for you how radical love alters our planet. Radical self-love is an internal process offering external transformation. How we show up to life reflects how we show up to ourselves. When we strip away the veneer of self-reliance and individualism and allow ourselves access to our most vulnerable truths, we can't help but be heartbeat present to the fact that our relationship with other bodies mirrors in tangible ways our relationship with our own body. Yes, we have been cutting and cruel to ourselves and have watched our internalized shame spill over into how we parent, how we manage employees, how we show up to friends and family. Yes, we believed that our bodies were too big, too dark, too pale, too scarred, too ugly, so we tucked, folded, hid ourselves away and wondered why our lives looked infinitesimally smaller than what we knew we were capable of. Yes, we have been less vibrant employees, less compassionate neighbors, less tolerant of the bodies of others, not because we are bad people but because we are guilty of each of those counts against ourselves.

Our lens to the outside world is an interior lens projecting our experience in our bodies onto our external landscape. A shame-clouded interior lens can only project shame and judgment. Employing a radical self-love ethos is like squirting Windex on our daily lives: suddenly we can see ourselves as employees or em-

> **Radical Reflection**
> *The least compassionate politician and the most rigid authority figure are demonstrating to us how they are with themselves. We can practice compassion for them while demanding accountability from them.*

ployers, as parents and friends, as neighbors and community members, as leaders, thinkers, doers—as humans, distinctly connected to other humans. Applying radical self-love to each facet of these roles and responsibilities alters the very fabric of humanity, ultimately creating a more just, equitable, and compassionate world.

## Speaking French and Implicit Bias

Bridging the gap between radical self-love and radical human love may feel like a Herculean task. "Sonya, it is hard enough to try this radical self-love stuff on myself! Now you want me to love the world?" What I am proposing is that radical human love is not an altruistic endeavor. We want a world that works for our bodies. There is one superhighway free of the debris of body shame and terror that gets us there, and that is radical human love. This means we must become the architects of a world that works for everybody and every body. Our responsibility to humanity is to unearth the ways in which we have been sabotaging the blueprints and thwarting the radical self-love efforts of others.

Right this minute, we are sauntering across someone's radical self-love path like a lumbering bovine. Removing ourselves as a barrier to other folks' radical self-love only becomes possible when we are willing to fear-facingly examine our beliefs. It is not enough to transform our relationship with our physical and emotional selves and leave the world around us unexamined or unaltered. Messages we received about the validity and invalidity of our own bodies did not occur in a vacuum. We were simultaneously receiving and spreading those messages. Dismantling oppression and our role in it demands that we explore where we have been complicit in the system of body terrorism while employing the same compassion we needed to explore our complicity in our internalized body shame. Regrettably, this is where too many of us choose to exit the radical self-love train. We desperately want our good intentions and niceness to be enough. Although each of us is inherently "enough" to be loved, valued, cared for, and treated with respect, our efforts to raze systems of oppression and injustice will require more than our niceness. "But I am a good person; I am nice to everyone" has never toppled one systemic inequity nor interrupted the daily acts of body terrorism leveled against humans throughout history. *You* are enough. Being good or nice is not.

---

### Unapologetic Inquiry #22

*Think of three times when your choice to be "nice" or "polite"
made you complicit in body shame or body terrorism.*

---

Why do we avoid looking at the ways in which we uphold systems of body shame and terror? For the exact same reasons we avoid exploring uncomfortable thoughts about our own bodies and lives: we are in a constant struggle to distinguish our indoctrinated beliefs and behaviors from our true, radically self-loving beings. Remember that we are not the sum of our thoughts or even actions. When we fail to make that distinction, we avoid exploring our ideas and continue to cause harm to ourselves and others. Seeing our thoughts and behaviors as part and not the whole of us allows us to transform our way of being with other bodies. In my "Ten Tools for Radical Self-Love" workshops, I describe our unconscious collusion with the system of body terrorism using the example of French.

If you were born into a francophone family, at around six to eight months of age you would utter your first mumbling word. Likely it would be *mère* (mother) or *père* (father). Your language would be an extension of the world around you, which would likely consist of your French-speaking primary caregivers. Between eighteen months and two years of age, you would develop sentences. Again, those sentences would reflect the language you had been immersed in since birth. Unless your caregivers spoke or regularly exposed you to other languages, you undoubtedly would still be speaking French, even without ever having picked up a book or taken a single class. You would become a fluent French speaker. As you were exposed to more information, resources, and social systems, all in French, you would gain even greater proficiency. Your default language would be French. You'd think your thoughts in French. If you desired to learn a new language, you would have to study it, take classes, practice speaking it with others who had aptitude. It would take effort. On occasion, despite your new linguistic pursuits, you would return to speaking French. You might even subconsciously translate the new language back to French. Likely, no matter how proficient you became in another language, even if you stopped speaking French altogether, sometimes you would still think in French.

Body terrorism is our universal native tongue, our French. We learned the language in our formative years. We were the small child in the grocery store from Chapter 2, learning the language of ableism and being taught by our mothers to scurry off and whisper in shame and secrecy about the disabled body. We were five-year-old ballerinas in dance class being told by our teacher that we must wear nude tights with our leotards, only to discover that the default for "nude" in every store was pink or tan, never brown. It was in that class that we learned the default hierarchy of white bodies. We were children in the school cafeteria singing "Fatty, fatty, two by four, can't fit through the kitchen door." Or chanting "Keisha, Keisha Bald Spots" on the bus. Whether we chanted and sang along or not, we knew with certainty that we never wanted to be the people in those bodies being targeted. We learned the language of fatphobia and weight stigma, the language of difference-shaming. We were becoming fluent in body terrorism, either as perpetrators or as inactive bystanders, not because we were bad people but because we were in an immersion school of body shame. As adults, we have likely done much to disengage from the overtly callous messages we received about many bodies. But without an intentional free dive into the subconscious ways in which we still adhere to those beliefs, enact them in our lives, and project them onto the bodies of others, we will continue to speak body terrorism—ahem, French— whether we want to or not.

> ### Radical Reflection
> *When we practice awareness, we will notice that we "speak French" all day long. "What is that person wearing? She is too big to wear that!" "He needs to stop being such a wimp." The only way to stop speaking French is to notice when we are.*

Researchers have a term for the phenomenon I'm describing with my French analogy: implicit bias. The term refers to the "attitudes or stereotypes that affect our understanding, actions, and decisions in an unconscious manner."[1] Implicit bias can be favorable or unfavorable, but its key component is that it is involuntary: without an individual's conscious awareness or control. If you are prone to a heightened need for control, the concept of implicit bias might make your head explode. "What do you mean I am thinking things I don't think I'm thinking?" I know it can be maddening. Our brains are highly sophisticated organs encoding trillions of responses that control everything from scratching your head to jumping when someone startles you. Our embedded behaviors are so vast it would be impossible to notice them all. However, we do have the ability to raise some of these functions to conscious awareness.

Early on we discussed the theory of in-group out-group bias. This theory can help us understand the origins of implicit bias and see its interruption as a pivotal tool in dismantling a world of body terrorism. Humans are predisposed to social categorization. We subconsciously evaluate who is part of our group and who is not. These assignments happen within seconds, directing our subsequent engagement and influencing our treatment of others. These biases most generously benefit the bodies we consider "normal" while fettering millions of folks on the path of radical self-love. None of us are solely culprits or solely victims. We all get a bit of what we give. Each person in a society is obstructing someone's road to radical self-love while simultaneously being obstructed on their own road. Unexamined implicit bias upholds the hierarchy of bodies in our society, reaffirming our system of default bodies and codifying structures of body-based oppression. Implicit bias proves that just as we have internalized messages of body shame, so too have we been willful and unintentional agents of body terrorism. Through the exploration of how body shame has obstructed our own path, and by making a personal commitment to the creation of a just and compassionate world, we open up to the fear-facing examination of how our indoctrination has hindered the paths of others. Systems and structures of body terrorism are constructed, governed, and operated by humans—that is (cough, cough), by us. We built them, and only our intentional, concentrated efforts to deconstruct body terrorism in ourselves and in our world will tear them down.

## Beating Body Terrorism from the Inside Out

Describing body terrorism as a systemic and structural issue underscores how our political, economic, and social systems uphold the marginalization of bodies based on race, gender, age, size, ability, sexual orientation, and a variety of other markers.

---

### Unapologetic Inquiry #23

*Destroying the system of body terrorism requires an investigation into our unconscious beliefs about other bodies. Remember, we are not our beliefs. We can examine them without judgment and shame. From a place of curiosity and compassion, explore the social, culture, and political messages you have received about the bodies listed below. How have those messages informed your relationship with those bodies?*

- *Fat bodies*
- *Bodies of other races*
- *Lesbian or gay bodies*
- *Transgender bodies*
- *Disabled bodies*
- *Aging bodies*
- *Bodies with mental illness*

---

Bodies are not the only designators of oppression, but all oppression is enacted on the body. To discuss oppression as a manifestation of body terrorism is to move the conversation out of the abstract and return it to its site of impact, the body. Otherwise we risk forgetting that oppression in its many variations is a shared experience. Everybody with a body is affected. Understanding body terrorism as a function of systems and structures does not abdicate our responsibility for working toward its eradication. We do not get to say, "Oh well, racism/sexism/ weight stigma/ageism/homophobia/transphobia/etc. is just so big. Boy, I sure hope 'they' figure it out." Systems do not maintain themselves; even our lack of intervention is an act of maintenance. Every structure in every society is upheld by the active and passive assistance of other human beings.

Let's take the example of body terrorism in the form of ableism. One structural manifestation of ableism is access. If you rented a space for an event and never considered whether that space had ramps, elevators, or disability restrooms, you would be individually upholding the system of ableism by not ensuring that a person with a disability could access your event. No, you didn't build the inaccessible building, but you did rent it, never considering its accessibility for all bodies, thus furthering the erasure of people with physical disabilities and their needs. The architects, investors, and builders who failed to include accessible accommodations for the building project participated in upholding the structural system of ableism by creating a barrier to access for people with disabilities in public life. Each of us is responsible for a sphere of influence. We are lawyers, salesclerks, teachers, loan officers, physicians, customer service representatives, counselors, judges, law enforcement agents— an inexhaustible list of humans whose jobs impact the lives of other humans every single day. As a human in a body sharing this planet with other humans in bodies, I have a responsibility to interrupt body terrorism, as do you.

This responsibility is distinct from some sort of savior complex in which radical self-love emboldens you to save the poor and downtrodden of Earth. Radical self-love is a manifestation of our interdependence. Lilla Watson, an Aboriginal Australian artist and activist, along with the activists of 1970s Queensland are credited with saying, "If you have come to help me, you are wasting your time. If you have come because your liberation is bound up with mine, then let us work together."[2] Our freedom from body terrorism is bound together. We each have a role in dismantling its systems and structures if we desire a free and spacious road to radical self-love. The first step is to interrupt the ways in which body terrorism resides in us.

## Changing Hearts

Civil and labor rights activist Grace Lee Boggs died in 2015, leaving a legacy of work that exemplified her willingness to fear-facingly wrestle with how we create sustainable social change and justice. As a philosopher, she grappled with the delineation between rebellion and revolution. Her exploration of these nuances led her to focus her later writings on what she saw as an unyielding connection between our personal transformation and a transformed world. She wrote:

> Being a victim of oppression in the United States is not enough to make you revolutionary, just as dropping out of your mother's womb is not enough to make you human. People who are full of hate and anger against their oppressors or who only see Us versus Them can make a rebellion but not a revolution. . . . Therefore, any group that achieves power, no matter how oppressed, is not going to act differently from their oppressors as long as they have not confronted the values that they have internalized and consciously adopted different values.[3]

Boggs tells us that the only sustainable foundation for a changed world is internal transformation. We need look no further than our present political and social realities to see this premise in action. Social uprisings and upheaval are ineradicable foundations of human history.

Laws, rules, and institutions are impermanent and fragile. They have been written, revised, and removed thousands of times over, and yet each new attempt at social change seems to be a mutation of a previous system of body terrorism. The PBS documentary *Slavery by Another Name* describes the post–Civil War practice of convict leasing: a system of leasing incarcerated people to local planters or industrialists in exchange for a minimal fee plus food and board.[4] Low initial cost to the people doing the leasing and increased revenue to the local prisons ballooned the practice, and soon wealthy entrepreneurs were buying and selling convicts between themselves. Laws like the "Black Codes" restricted Black life and freedom while disproportionately targeting Blacks for incarceration.[5] The body terrorism of slavery found its structural mutation in the form of convict leasing and Jim Crow laws. Today, mass incarceration serves the same function, according to legal scholar and author Michelle Alexander. She details the comparison in her groundbreaking book *The New Jim Crow:*

> In the era of colorblindness, it is no longer socially permissible to use race, explicitly, as a justification for discrimination, exclusion, and social contempt. So, we don't. Rather than rely on race, we use our criminal justice system to label people of color "criminals" and then engage in all the practices we supposedly left behind. Today it is perfectly legal to discriminate against criminals in nearly all the ways that it was once legal to discriminate against African Americans. Once you're labeled a felon, the old forms of discrimination—employment discrimination, housing discrimination, denial of the right to vote, denial of educational opportunity, denial of food stamps and other public benefits, and exclusion from jury service—are suddenly legal. As a criminal, you have scarcely more rights, and arguably less respect, than a black man living in Alabama at the height of Jim Crow. We have not ended racial caste in America; we have merely redesigned it.[6]

Shortly after being inaugurated U.S. president, Donald Trump signed a series of executive orders targeting Muslims and Latinos. The orders ranged from banning visa holders from seven mostly Muslim countries, to blocking the acceptance of Syrian refugees, to ordering a wall built on the border of Mexico, to increasing immigration raids on undocumented families.[7] These actions emboldened national racism and xenophobia and harkened to a long history of state-sanctioned body terrorism. The Chinese Exclusion Act of 1882 placed a decade-long moratorium on the immigration of Chinese people into the United States, with the result of scapegoating them for the country's economic woes and limiting their rights for the next fifty years. Citing fears of Nazi spies, Franklin D. Roosevelt drastically limited the number of Jewish refugees allowed into the country during World War II, taking less than a quarter of the twenty-six thousand he had authorized annually. This decision meant that in June 1939 the ocean liner SS *St. Louis,* which carried nearly one thousand Jewish passengers, was turned away from multiple ports and forced to return to Europe. More than a quarter of its passengers are believed to have been killed in the Holocaust.[8]

We do not have to travel far back through history to describe the shape-shifting nature of body terrorism. Homophobia and xenophobia led to an immigration ban in the United States against HIV-positive persons. The ban remained in place for more than two decades (until 2009), sanctioning social stigma and embedding it into foreign policy.[9] These legal and political decisions illuminate that shape-shifting power of centuries of body terrorism.

Why do we keep reinventing new forms of body terrorism? To answer that question let's explore a conversation between former presidential candidate Hillary Clinton and a group of Black Lives Matter activists that took place in New Hampshire during the 2015 primaries. In a reportedly tense meeting, the soon-to-be Democratic nominee chided the young activists for what she saw as a naïve

and unrealistic approach to addressing police violence against un-
armed Black citizens. "Look, I don't believe you change hearts,"
Clinton said, arguing that the movement couldn't change deep-
seated racism. "I believe you change laws, you change allocation of
resources, you change the way systems operate. You're not going to
change every heart. You're not."[10] Certainly, candidate Clinton felt
she was offering sage advice at the time, highlighting the dangers of
placing idealism above political pragmatism. Surprisingly, a year
later Clinton released a campaign video in collaboration with the
Human Rights Campaign that opens with her stating, "Equality is,
of course, about changing laws, but it's also about changing hearts
and minds."[11] Perhaps the final year on the campaign trail gave Hillary
a peek into the true social and cultural consequences of our historical unwillingness to work to change hearts. Failing to change hearts
makes body terrorism a centuries-old shell game of guessing what
new law it is hiding beneath now.

Juan Manuel Montes was a twenty-three-year-old undocumented
immigrant who, despite being protected under the Deferred Action
for Childhood Arrivals (DACA) program, was deported in early
2017 to Mexico, a country he had not lived in since age nine.[12] Body
terrorism is not a historical aberration, it is the lived experience
of millions of people at this very moment. As Chinese immigrants,
Jews turned away at port, Leelah Acorn, and Juan Manuel Montes
would tell you if they could, the consequences of unchanged hearts
are life and death. Body terrorism is made of both systems and structures, hearts and minds. It is the constant stratification of bodies,
placing us into hierarchies where we are valued and denigrated often
at the same time, in the same body. Propagating a world of radical
self-love is both a practice of individual transformation and a commitment to collective transformation. It is a practice of personal and
global thinking, doing, and being. Radical self-love necessitates

changed hearts, beginning with our own. Quite simply, we cannot build in the world that which we have not built in ourselves.

## Unapologetic Agreements

Moving from a radical self-love that transforms you to a radical love that creates justice and equity in the world may feel like a tall order, but you are already on your way. As we cultivate new ways of being in our own bodies, we develop new ways of *being* on this planet with other bodies. A return to radical self-love requires our commitment to building shame-free, inclusive communities that uplift one another while honestly addressing body terrorism in all the ways it manifests as oppression based on age, race, gender, size, ability, sexual orientation, mental health status, and all other human attributes. Some will deride our efforts with charges of playing to "identity politics." We should remind those people that they, too, have identities that are informed by their bodies. Their lack of awareness about those identities generally means their body falls into a multiplicity of default identities that uphold the social hierarchy of bodies. The luxury of not having to think about one's body always comes at another body's expense. We should, with compassion, remind them that oppression oppresses us all, even those who are default. Not even they will always have a body at the top of the ladder. No one wins in a world of body terrorism.

At this very moment someone is wringing their hands in worry. "But what if I make a mistake, Sonya? What if I say or do the wrong thing?" If it is you who are worrying, let me calm your precious nerves by assuring you that you will make a mistake . . . and then reminding you to revisit pillar 4. Creating a radical self-love world requires our willingness to have challenging conversations about privilege, power, history, culture, inequality, pain, and injustice. We will mess up and say something in French. That doesn't mean we quit. It also doesn't mean we become defensive and retreat to judgment and blame. It means we apologize and try again, holding fast to our intention to connect with other humans in different bodies from a place of compassion and shared humanity. As you move the conversation of radical self-love from an internal dialogue out into your family, community, and world, try on the Unapologetic Agreements that appear below. Commit to engaging in the type of radical self-love communication that grows our understanding of ourselves and one another—the type of communication that fosters global change.

1. **Be a body-shame-free friend.** Eliminate language that disparages bodies based on race, age, size, gender, ability, sexual orientation, religion, mental health status, or any other attribute. Compassionately challenge others you hear using body-shame language to describe themselves or others. This includes "health or concern trolling" (making unsolicited comments about a person's health based on their physical appearance).

2. **Engage and encourage curiosity-driven *dialogue*, not debate or arguing.** Practice the value of sharing and listening to the perspectives of others. The goal of dialogue need not be to change anyone's mind, but to *offer* and *receive* a perspective for consideration and curiosity.

3. **Embrace multiple perspectives.** Avoid having conversations from the assumption of right and wrong. Even if every cell in your body disagrees with someone's perspective, remember that making people "bad" and "wrong" will never build connection and understanding. People who feel judged and attacked often only become further entrenched in their ideas.[13]

4. **Have compassion for and honor people's varied journeys.** Not everyone has read the books you've read or had the experiences you've had. There was a time when you had not

had them either. Our journeys are unique and varied. Compassion births patience.

5. **Expect and accept discomfort.** Conversations about centuries-old oppressions are *hard!* If they were not, the world would be rid of body terrorism and oppression by now. Honor how we all have been indoctrinated into systems of oppression that we each must unlearn. Unlearning is challenging. Do not expect neat, tidy resolutions or assume that we will instantly "fix" the world's ills in a single dialogue. We can, however, get closer to those goals if we are willing to be uncomfortable. Remember, fear is not necessarily danger.

6. **Acknowledge intent while addressing impact.** It is possible to be well-meaning and still cause harm. No matter our intention, we practice accountability when we are willing to acknowledge the impact of our words and actions on others. Likewise, people's words and behaviors may have an impact on us, but they are rarely actually about us. The way we respond to situations is most often a reflection of our own journey. Refraining from personalization makes accepting discomfort easier.

7. **Take breaks for self-care.** Talking with friends, family, and community about radical self-love, body terrorism, and body shame can be joyous and eye-opening. It can also be challenging and triggering. These conversations often involve issues that have caused great trauma in the world—and in our own lives. Some dialogues may bring up painful memories, old wounds, present hurts, and current resentments. We place a premium on self-care as a tool of radical self-love! Do what you need to do to navigate your mental, emotional, and physical well-being. Step away from conversations when needed. Focus on yourself, and come back when you are recentered. Radical self-love dialogue depends on your wellness.

8. **Interrupt attempts to derail.** Oftentimes, conversations about body terrorism and oppression bring up such discomfort that we immediately attempt to change the conversation to something that feels more comfortable. Before you know it, the conversation turns to pickle farmers in Europe when we started out talking about fat shaming. Work to keep the focus on the subject being addressed, and avoid the desire to derail.

9. **Remember that personal attacks, name-calling, heavy sarcasm, and general unkindness are unhelpful.** The fastest way to devolve a dialogue is to turn to mean or hurtful language. Our anger need not be expressed as cruelty. We should work to speak from our "inside voice."

10. **Practice unapologetic inquiry.** Part of helping people sort through their ideas and beliefs is to ask questions about those ideas. That includes asking *ourselves* hard questions: "Why do I believe this? What am I afraid of? What am I gaining or losing by trying on a new perspective?" The answers that stick with us over time are the answers we come up with ourselves. Good questions get us to good answers.

11. **Have conversations based on what was actually said.** Often our translations of people's ideas are not accurate depictions of what they were sharing. Be sure to engage with people based on their actual words and not what you assume those words meant. If you are unsure, ask for clarity.

12. **Assume the best about one another.** It is exceptionally painful to be dismissed, called a liar, or accused of making up your experiences. Start from the assumption that people's experiences are *real* and that they are the expert on their experience. We *may* have shared experiences, but this is not always true. Ask to learn more about other people's truths, rather than erasing them. Start from the assumption that we are all doing our best at any given moment with the tools we have.

13. **Celebrate difference.** Identifying difference is a way to embrace how we can all show up as our fullest, most authentic selves without shame. Acknowledge and embrace those things that are varied in us. Notice when difference is absent, and interrogate why. Ask who is not in the room. Our love of difference translates into creating a movement that welcomes everybody and every body.

14. **Make the goal of the conversation radical, unapologetic love.** The desire for a world free of body terrorism is a desire born out of love. Activist Che Guevara once said, "At the risk of seeming ridiculous, let me say that the true revolutionary is guided by a great feeling of love."[14] Allow your conversations to be guided by the primary principle of love.

"Sonya, will following these agreements keep me from arguing with my racist, fatphobic Aunt Martha during Thanksgiving dinner?" Listen, love, I cannot promise that you will never again storm out of the house and finish your holiday meal at the local Denny's. However, I can tell you that I have seen the Unapologetic Agreements transform hostility into human connection and acrimony into camaraderie. Like all radical self-love principles, they will take time and effort to master. But keep working at it. "You will be amazed before you are even halfway through."[15]

# 5

# Your Radical Self-Love Toolkit

## You Are Not a Car

Some of us, before this whole conversation about radical self-love, didn't so much hate our bodies as we engaged them like they were vehicles, like a car we drove around. We paid only as much attention as was absolutely necessary to get the car started and get on with our day. We put gas in the car so we didn't end up stuck on the side of a deserted highway or on some backwoods road out of a horror film. We occasionally took the car to the shop if it seemed like something extreme was up. Sometimes we trashed the car, littering the passenger seats with wrappers and water bottles. Some of us went for months without visiting a car wash. We would awaken, get in our cars, and go, navigating our lives while giving very little thought to our vehicles until we needed them again.

This model was not sustainable. There are some key differences between a car and your body, the primary one being that should you wake up and find that your car won't start, you will either (1) buy a new car, or (2) find a new mode of transportation. Should you find that your body won't start, we can safely assume you didn't wake up. To treat our bodies like cars is to essentially treat ourselves like something disposable. You, my love, are not disposable. Besides, your body wants nothing more than to be your buddy through this ride called life, and that means you need a solid set of tools for the road.

## Ten Tools for Radical Self-Love

Over the last four chapters we have laid out the concepts and theories that undergird a radical self-love framework. We've combed the innermost realms of our beliefs, illuminated the structural and systemic biases of our societies, excavated our personal body shames and judgments, and contemplated a planet without body terrorism. Awesome! But radical self-love is not merely conceptual; it must be practical if it is to be transformative. The four pillars of practice offered us a thinking, doing, and being model for leading a radically self-loving life. Associated with each pillar are specific tools and practices you can begin working on today to revolutionize the way you live and love in your body.

### *Pillar 1: Taking Out the Toxic*

#### Tool 1: Dump the Junk

On any given day we may find ourselves in our local grocery store waiting in line to buy organic kale chips, when we feel the energetic tug of the current fashion or tabloid magazine calling to us from just above the Orbit gum. Of course we want to know why Kim Kardashian put hubby Kanye West out of the house last week, and of course we need to know the Five Secrets to Solving the Sin of Cellulite. Before we are even consciously aware of it, we are handing the cashier a twenty-dollar bill for kale chips, Kim K, and diet tips. Getting sucked into the vortex of escapism is alluring. Wanting to dive headfirst into anyone's life besides our own is certainly understandable, but that mini mental vacation is not without cost. The content we are exposed to impacts us. Whether we like it or not, we are taking in toxic messages.

Is the answer to swear off all media and adopt a monastic life? No, not unless you are into that sort of thing. But we can be intentional about the media we ingest, and we certainly do not have to give our hard-fought dollars to industries that profit from self-hate and body terrorism. "Dump the Junk" is a tool for detoxifying our daily lives from mass-media body shame. Ducking every awful message lobbed at us via television, radio, and internet is unrealistic. We are humans living in the world. Nevertheless, we can be intentional and strategic about how we engage with media. Toxic media creates a cumulative effect of body shame that erodes our sense of self and places a scrim of distrust and scrutiny on the bodies of others over time. Dumping the junk turns down the high-decibel volume of body-negative messages, creating some space for us to assess our own bodies and the bodies of others with less background noise.

> ### Unapologetic Inquiry #24
>
> *Do you feel unsure exactly how much body-shame and body-terrorism content you are absorbing weekly? To sort through the static, try on this question: what am I watching that contributes to the oppression of my body by making bodies like it bad, wrong, a joke, invisible, dehumanized, a caricature, shamed, etc.?*

To actively dump the junk, consider a media fast. Commit to one day per week when you actively choose not to engage in television, radio, or social media content that reaffirms negative messages about bodies. If you're flipping through the channels and land on *Real Housewives of Pluto* . . . change it. Reading a magazine with an ad for how to lose those "stubborn ten pounds" . . . set it down. Hearing radio ads offering you plastic surgery . . . turn it off. Do you have a job in which you must engage with the media? Spend time interrogating the messages. What is the content asking you to believe about your body? What is it asking you to believe about other folks' bodies? Notice your thinking after your media fast. How do your mind, body, and spirit feel? Fill your time with new areas of interest, complete unfinished projects, spend time with friends. You just gave yourself fifteen extra hours a week. That's what you call radical wealth!

## Tool 2: Curb Body Bad-Mouthing

Does the following scenario sound familiar? Two friends are in a clothing store trying on potential purchases, when friend 1 says, "OMG, I look like a cow in this!" In response to that self-effacing comment, friend 2 retorts, "No you don't. You look great! Now, *I* would look like a cow in that!" The two friends proceed to volley mutual accolades over fitting-room doors, all the while tossing darts of body insults at themselves. We call this friendship.

Our society has formed a sense of cultural camaraderie around body shame that dictates we affirm one another at the expense of ourselves. This is a menacing mechanism of body terrorism. In a society that applauds our ability to make ourselves literally and figuratively smaller, it is no surprise we employ this strategy within our social relationships. How often are we asked to shrink ourselves in size, presence, and power? To be bold and unapologetic is to quickly be maligned as cocky, arrogant, or worse. Couple this with the capi-

> **Radical Reflection**
> *Self-deprecation is valued as a sign of wit in today's culture. Comedians Louis C.K. and Amy Schumer have risen to great fame on the backs of their perceived flaws and inadequacies. Unfortunately, this brand of humor also makes it easier to make fun of others.*

talistic model of scarcity that supposes there is not enough money, space, time, or love for us all, and it is no wonder we find ourselves abdicating our personal power to uplift our friends. What happens when we toss out that tired model and stand unapologetically in our power? We not only embolden ourselves but also inspire those we love to do the same.

Singer/songwriter Jill Scott did exactly that in the concert documentary *Dave Chappelle's Block Party.*[1] In the film, Scott is being interviewed by a reporter in the green room while her industry peer Erykah Badu is lighting up the stage with her performance. The reporter and Jill gush over Badu for a moment, praising her prowess. Then the reporter asks Scott whether she's nervous in light of the fact that she must follow Badu's performance. Jill Scott's response was as apple-pie sweet as it was guillotine swift: "Have you ever seen me perform?"

Scott did not see shirking her power or shrinking her talent as a prerequisite for appreciating and supporting a fellow artist. She was unapologetically clear that owning her gifts in no way diminished Badu's. Radical self-love does not call on us to be less of ourselves. Radical self-love summons us to be our most expansive selves, knowing that the more unflinchingly powerful we allow ourselves to be, the more unflinchingly powerful others feel capable of being. Our unapologetic embrace of our bodies gives others permission to unapologetically embrace theirs.

How we speak about our bodies impacts how we experience our bodies. Language can be a tool for body terrorism or a tool for radical self-love. Pejoratively using words like *fat* entrenches body shame into our psyches, impacting how we see and treat fat bodies. But it doesn't have to be this way. Body activist, author, and fabulous friend Jes Baker articulates this sentiment in her book *Things No One Will Tell Fat Girls*:

Saying I'm fat is (and should be) the same as saying my shoes are black, the clouds are fluffy, and Bob Saget is tall. It's not good, it's not bad, it just is. The only negativity that this word carries is that which has been socially constructed around it. . . . We don't need to stop using the word *fat*, we need to stop the hatred that our world connects with the word *fat*.[2]

Curbing body bad-mouthing is the perfect tool for moving our self-deprecating language from the default of constantly running background noise to a body-shame language we recognize and interrupt as often as possible.

---

### Unapologetic Inquiry #25

*Notice the words you use to describe yourself negatively. Which words do you hear others using as insults? Consider words like* fat, crazy, gay, black, blind. *Keep track of how often you casually use these terms. Make a list of some body-shame-free alternatives.*

---

## Pillar 2: Mind Matters

### Tool 3: Reframe Your Framework

Did you know that your body is not the enemy? I know how difficult this concept can be when we feel as though we have been at war with our bodies for our entire existence, but this is a case of friendly fire, folks, and we are usually the shooters. Think back to your last cold or flu. Chills, fever, scratchy throat, fatigue, that crusty stuff that builds around your . . . you get the picture. Awful, right? And it is our mean old body's fault! After all, the body is working overtime to disperse those white blood cells to the site of the virus, attempting to squash its insidious attack on our immune system! Awful, mean old body, right? Wrong. Feeling crappy when we're sick is not a sign of a body that is mutinying; it's the unfortunate byproduct of a body working exponentially hard to return us to wellness. Our body is fighting on our behalf even as we curse it as though it were a cheating lover. Practicing "Reframe Your Framework" can be confounding for those of us navigating chronic illness or gender nonconformity. Feeling trapped in a body that does not feel like it has your best interest at heart assuredly makes sense. It is hard to love a vessel that appears to be the author of significant pain. What a terrifying experience to wake up in constant pain or in a body that does not feel in alignment with who you know yourself to be. It may very well feel like your body is against you. Remember that this is a thinking, doing, being journey, and we will need to try on new beliefs and actions in the service of radical self-love. With tool 3 in mind, we are invited to ask ourselves, "What peace, power, or joy can be gained by deciding that this body I am inextricably tied to for the rest of my life is my enemy?" If there is no access to peace, power, or joy in your current framework, then it simply doesn't serve you.

In a 2015 article on the website XOJane, author and clinical social worker Kai Cheng Thom pens what she calls "a love letter between a woman and her body." She challenges the pervasive narrative of being a transwoman "born in the wrong body." She writes, "I began to see that my body was not the cause of the hatred directed against me—society did that. My body did not fail to protect me when I was attacked; I did not deserve violence. My body has never been wrong. Someone else decided that."[3] Kai Cheng Thom grasped that by trying on a new framework, it was possible to "relate to my body, transform my body, from a place of joy instead of anger and fear."

Radical self-love asks us to try on new ways of thinking and doing that give us access to new ways of being. Trying on a new framework is like trying on a new coat. It may or may not fit. The coat isn't wrong for not fitting. You are not wrong for not fitting in the coat. It just doesn't fit. Far too many of us have been walking around the world wearing our "my body is the enemy" coat, wondering why we feel trapped and miserable. We tried on a thinking that doesn't fit our pursuit of radical self-love. Deciding our body is the enemy leaves us fighting an unwinnable battle on our own soil. It all comes down to a simple question: if you decide to be at war with your body, how will you ever have peace?

### Unapologetic Inquiry #26

*Consider the ways in which you have been at war with your body. How have you tried to fight your body or make it surrender to your will? How have you shown it animosity? How can you practice radical reconciliation?*

**Tool 4: Meditate on a Mantra**
Do you have a "right now," a "someday," or a "remember back when" relationship with your body? Imagine waiting on a subway platform for a train that is due in five minutes, except it's eight hours later and the train has never come. You have missed an entire work day! Waiting for the train has become an excuse for doing nothing while declaring, "I swear, someday that train is going to come." At this point the night staff is locking up the place around you.

Now, imagine you are running to catch the train, and as you arrive on the platform it pulls away. Instead of catching the next train, you stand there for eight hours lamenting how you just missed that stupid train. Thirty trains have passed since you arrived, and yet there you are, shivering and alone in the dark, reminiscing about when you almost caught that damn train! In both scenarios one thing remains true: you are stuck on the platform of life, not going anywhere. Whether you are waiting for the wealth train, the weight loss train, or the new-lover train to take you to happiness or you are watching the "remember when I weighed 125 pounds" train leave with all your joy, your most amazing life is not happening on the train you missed or the one that didn't arrive. You are avoiding life. Life is happening right now. Tool 4 is designed to get us off that platform and back to a "right now" relationship with our bodies.

Meditation calls on us to be present in the immediate moment, the right now. Meditating asks us to notice what sensations, pleasant or unpleasant, are arising in our bodies, not for the sake of eradicating them but to simply make peace with our present state. Miraculously, through the process of meditation, unpleasant states dissipate on their own. We don't even have to try to make them go away. A 2016 study done by the Carnegie Mellon University Health and Human Performance Laboratory recruited thirty-five unemployed men and women who were seeking work and experiencing considerable stress. After taking baseline diagnostic medical information, researchers taught half the subjects formal mindfulness meditation (open, receptive, nonjudgmental awareness of your present-moment experience). The rest of the participants were taught a made-up method that focused on relaxation and distraction from worry. When the study concluded, all thirty-five participants claimed to feel less stress and a greater sense of ease. However, brain scans showed that members of the group that practiced mindfulness meditation had greater activity in the regions of the brain responsible for processing stress-related actions, for the sense of calm, and for communication. Four months later, those who practiced mindfulness meditation demonstrated "much lower levels in their blood of a marker of unhealthy inflammation than the relaxation group, even though few were still meditating."[4] Meditation alters our physical and emotional state. It also turns down the volume on body shame.

Our brains are cunning and resilient, storing decades' worth of information for the sake of keeping us alive. As is true of our social media profiles, there are upsides and downsides to having that much information stockpiled in one place. We are hardwired to retain negative experiences.[5] This cognitive function is why we haven't intentionally touched a hot stove since we were three or used Aqua Net hairspray since we were fifteen. We are biologically predisposed to remember painful things as a function of evolution. These experiences form the informational autobahns of our brains—our neuropathways. This is where mantras come in. A mantra is a word or phrase used repetitively. In Sanskrit, *mantra* means a tool or instrument of the mind. Mantras not only soothe us but when used in conjunction with meditation can reroute the neuropathways of our brains by replacing negative thought patterns with new ideas—radical self-love ideas.[6] Choosing a mantra is about finding a phrase or word we desire to live by. It should make us uncomfortable. It should make us think, "How dare I believe such an audacious thing about myself?" If you feel a little queasy when you speak your mantra aloud, you have probably found the right one. Your mantra should feel like your growing edge. A good mantra may make your body-shame voice louder at first. This is a good sign. Mantras that challenge our current neurological pathways of body shame will initially trigger those pathways as we endeavor to disrupt them. Here are a few mantras you may want to try:

- I love my body.
- I am a vessel of radical self-love.
- My body is my ally.
- I have the body I need to live my best life.

Practice meditating five minutes a day for thirty days and see what happens. Invite the discomfort of sitting in the stillness of the present and saying words you do not yet truly believe. I promise that radical self-love transformation will be birthed in the quiet of those vexatious moments. Meditating on a mantra reminds us that it is time get off that subway platform and get to living. Life is not behind us or before us. Our most amazing, unapologetic life is right here, right now!

---

### Unapologetic Inquiry #27

*Our brains are wired for trillions of functions. However, they do not have to stay routed on an express train of body shame and hatred. We can reroute our mental address to radical self-love. Using the following questions, craft two affirmative mantras that you can live into:*

1. *If I were free of shame or discomfort, what might I say about my body?*
2. *If I were unafraid of failure or disappointment, what would I do right now?*

---

## Tool 5: Banish the Binary

Humans have developed myriad ways to organize the vast quantity of information we take in every day. We categorize life like we separate laundry: lights, darks, gentle cycle, permanent press. But much like laundry, life doesn't always fall into neat and easily definable categories. Neither do we. We are messy, we humans. We are plaid and polka dot, silk and denim—all in the same shirt. We are hard to sort out. Which is why binary thinking doesn't serve our radical self-love journey. Historically, we have used the term *binary* to talk about number sequences, a land reserved for statisticians and computer coders.[7] A more contemporary treatment of the term deals with our often rigid and dualistic understanding of gender as strictly male or female, feminine or masculine, and attracted to men or women based solely on those assignments.[8] This inflexibility erases the nuance and diversity of human gender and sexuality. Furthermore, binary thinking, when expanded to include all the ways we marginalize the gradients of human behavior and identity, illuminates how either/ or thinking limits the fullness of our human potential and clouds our radical self-love vision.

We are not simply good or bad; vessels of pure, divine light or mongers of hate; interrupters of body terrorism everywhere or single-handedly upholding the oppression of bodies across the planet. If "good" and "bad" were the choices on a quiz about who we are, the answer would be "all of the above." Humans (i.e., you and I) are doing and being all those things all the time. If human behavior were charted on a scatter graph, we each would have dots on every portion of the spectrum: in the middle, at the ends, and every place in between. Binary thinking limits our possibility, squelches compassion, and re-inforces narrow ideas of how we get to "be" in the world. That marginalization is a function of internalized body terrorism. If you recall, the practice of "I am not my thoughts" prompted us to examine our thoughts from a place of curiosity and diminished judgment. The same is true for our behaviors. We can change our behaviors, but only when we see them as mutable—*of* us but *not* us. Honor that you will be many things throughout the course of your life. Sometimes you will be a phenomenal gift; sometimes you will get on someone's damn nerves. There is gorgeous potential and heinous instinct in us all. Singularity does not define us. Our instincts influence and shape us but do not define us. When we find ourselves in the land of either/or thinking—characterized by words like *never, always, only, every time, mostly,*

> **Radical Reflection**
> *Humans aren't laundry! Stop trying to compartmentalize and sort yourself out. Messy does not always mean dirty. Sometimes it just means complicated, and complicated can be beautiful! Ask yourself, "How might I approach life differently if I had compassion for my beautiful mess?"*

*rarely*—it is a great sign that we may be off our path. Binary thinking is the antithesis of radical self-love.

## Pillar 3: Unapologetic Action

### Tool 6: Explore Your Terrain

My life partner is a six-pound Yorkshire terrier named Anastasia Duchess. Adopted at eight weeks old, she has been my constant companion and adorable rabble-rouser. Part of the responsibility of choosing her as a life partner was committing to an intimacy unlike anything I had experienced prior. In our first month together, I had to squeeze a tick from her belly, remove impacted stool from her butt, and be awakened by the fresh scent of puppy poop as she scooted her diarrhea-laden backside across my forehead while I slept. This was more intimacy and poop than I had ever known. Loving my dog was an outgrowth of caring for her. That care required that I get all up in the gross details of her little dog self so that I could identify the mundane but telling indicators of her health. By learning about and caring for her little body, I grew to love her profoundly.

We rarely allow ourselves this level of intimacy with our own bodies. Parts of us have gone unobserved, let alone touched, for decades. This negligence is not without cost. A 2003 National Health Industry Survey found that 57 percent of breast cancer survivors found their cancer through breast self-examination or by accident.[9] Put plainly, we must touch our bodies, in all manner of ways and for all manner of reasons. It is impossible to be a responsible steward of a body we constantly avoid being intimate with. Building love relationships require getting to know the other party. Our relationships with our bodies are no different. As we learn them, we can access their unique power and gifts.

A workshop participant whom I'll call Nicole shared how stuck she'd been feeling when she started working with this tool. Nicole's history of sexual trauma made touching herself an act filled with anxiety. I suggested that Nicole add structure to the process and focus her touch around specific intentions. Having a purpose, time, and intention for touching herself allowed her to choose which kind of touch she felt up for and gave her time to prepare emotionally for the experience. Over the course of several phone conversations, Nicole and I developed what I call the three E's of touch: exploration, examination, and ecstasy.

When we build intimacy with our bodies through the process of exploration, we are learning the topography of our flesh. What colors, shades, and textures make up our landscape? As we do in our meditation process, we allow ourselves simply to notice what is present with our bodies. Exploration gives us a baseline understanding of how our bodies look and feel. This baseline is the foundation for the second E, examination.

If exploration is like a MapQuest of our bodies (it tells us the basics), then examination is the app with real-time traffic updates. Understanding our unique terrain gives us access to awareness. With awareness, we can be alerted when something is off-kilter. Noticing skin discoloration or variations in our body mass gives us the information we need to advocate for our well-being. Doctors are fantastic, but they do not know your body better than you. Examination makes you an expert in you, and you should be.

Lastly, touch yourself for ecstasy. Our bodies are designed for pleasure, but so many of us deny ourselves the riches of our own sensual touch. A 2009 *Psychology Today* article reported on a comprehensive analysis of thirty-three studies of female orgasm over the preceding eighty years. The analysis was conducted by Elisabeth Lloyd, author of *The Case of the Female Orgasm*. She found that only about half of women sometimes have orgasms during intercourse. About 20 percent seldom or never have orgasms during intercourse. And about 5 percent never have orgasms, period.[10] Physiology is a key reason for the lack of female orgasm. Most orgasms are achieved through clitoral stimulation, and there is generally not enough friction during intercourse to generate arousal to orgasm. Know what might help such an issue? Touching yourself! When we touch ourselves sexually, we are not just getting ourselves off (which is wonderful); we are becoming masterful tour guides for our lovers. We know all the most breathtaking views and the best places to dine! Giving ourselves pleasure is a powerful way to teach others how to please us. Radical self-love is built on the foundation of intimacy with our bodies. Get intimate with your body and it will teach you and others how to love it.

---

### Unapologetic Inquiry #28

*Ecstasy is not a naughty word. Our bodies are designed for pleasure, and we should never feel ashamed about enjoying them. When was the last time you took a moment to explore pleasure in your body? Take five minutes and write down the four sensations your body enjoys the most. Only include things that do not require other people. Pick two of them, and do them! Then reflect on what it was like to intentionally indulge in the rapture of your gorgeous body.*

---

**Tool 7: Be in Movement**

Do you remember kindergarten recess? The bell rang, the teacher dismissed the class, and, if you were like me, you grew wings, levitated above your chair, and promptly flew out of the classroom, landing squarely on the hot black asphalt of the school yard. Before the playground became a site of body shame and terrorism, before crushes and elementary school politics, there were a swing set, tetherball, you, and ten to twenty other sweaty, gleeful little children. We loved recess because recess meant movement. After hours of being confined to those uncomfortable wooden desks, recess was body liberation. Movement was an axis of joy, not drudgery. Today, many of us move from a sense of shame or obligation, which generally means the movement doesn't last long. Every January, gyms spill over with new humans resolving to "get fit," drop fifteen pounds, or whatever the latest resolution is. By March, the gym is back to bare. Not because we are all lazy losers but because our commitments are birthed out of duress. We are at the gym because we're "supposed" to be, not because we legitimately enjoy it. We have a limited shelf life in these bodies, and, yes, we want to care for them as best we can. Exercise can be a positive activity, but good for us does not have to equal soul torture.

About three years ago, the voice of the dreaded "should" told me I needed to run a 5K. I wasn't even sure what the *K* in 5K stood for, but still, I downloaded the app and started to run. Mysteriously, that same loud "should" voice failed to remind me that jogging might not be the most comfortable medium of exercise for a person who wears a size 36JJ bra. Nevertheless, I found myself pounding the dirt trails of scenic northern California, sweat stinging my eyes, shoulders cracking beneath the weight of my ample bosom. Jogging made my teeth ache. Literally, my gums would throb with pain at the 2.5K mark of each run. About two weeks in, I was on the trail, hands affixed atop my breasts, trying to keep from giving myself a concussion, when my gums began the dull thud of pain that was common with every run. On this day I stopped, stood stock still, and asked myself, "Why in the hell am I doing this? I hate running!" Barely upright at the peak of an Oakland trail staring into the resplendent sunshine of San Francisco, I got honest with myself and my body. I didn't want to run. I didn't like it, and it was silly of me to force myself to do something that brought me zero joy. What I wanted to do was sign up for the West African dance class at my local community center and learn the Moribayasa, a dance for women overcoming great adversity (the perfect honor for my breasts). And that's exactly what I did: dropped the jogging and found some movement that made me happy. I assure you, my gums and my boobs thanked me.

How do we know that movement is an inherent joy? Because babies who are completely incapable of forming sentences or peeing in the pot move their bodies to music. Whether they're gyrating to hot Latin beats or mimicking Michael Jackson, babies remind us that our bodies are made for movement and that movement is an act of freedom and radical self-love. Find those babies on YouTube, and then find what moves you and go do it![11]

## Unapologetic Inquiry #29

*What were your favorite childhood games? Did you play kickball, Mother may I, red light/green light, capture the flag? Did you love to go walking along a creek or in the woods? Did you love swimming? Dancing? Why did you stop doing what delighted you? What might happen if you invited those activities back into your life? You still deserve to be delighted.*

**Tool 8: Make a New Story**

Our body shame is a story whose chapters began being written in some of our earliest memories. Body shame is not a thrilling page-turner but a grueling text of embarrassment, judgment, and grief. Our story made us believe we would never have love, we would never be good enough, we would always be rejected. Decades later we find ourselves still stuck, the body-shame story on loop in our minds. We do not have to keep that story. We absolutely have the power to turn in that cheap and tawdry tale and make a new story.

One the earliest followers of my blog, *The Body Is Not an Apology,* illustrated the transformative potential of choosing to make a new story. Julie was in her late twenties and of Sicilian descent, a heritage that she said explained the flowing ringlets of chestnut tresses that cascaded down her back. Being Sicilian also explained the wisps of ebony hair that coated her arms and snaked down her cheeks as sideburns. Julie was hairy and had spent years making peace with the birthright of her DNA, but she couldn't shake the deep sense of shame about having hair on her back. Julie had a story she was living in, parts of it given to her by mean children, portions passed down through razor commercials and messages of hairlessness as a standard of femininity. All these contributors had written chapters in a book that was making Julie miserable. Remember, I said discomfort is a catalyst for change. We keep our body-shame stories for such long periods of time because their pain is familiar. It is comfortable. When we awaken to the ideas of radical self-love, body shame becomes an uncomfortable residence and we are called to move. Julie's discomfort prompted her to act; she decided to make a new story, literally. One day, over a latte in a coffee shop in Colorado, Julie shared her new story with me.

### Julie's Story

In a far-off land beyond the clouds, angel children dwelled among the gods awaiting assignment to be born. Each angel child was given a choice of the parents they would like to be born to. These assignments were based on the lessons the angel child most needed to master in their time on Earth. Angel child Julie had recently chosen her soon-to-be parents and was preparing to leave the land of angel children to be conceived on Earth. The gods summoned Julie to share with her the details of her assignment and to collect her wings. Julie never considered that she would not be allowed to keep her wings when she left the land of angel children, and she was inconsolable when the gods informed her. She cried ceaselessly every day until the final moment she left the land of angel children. The gods felt tender sadness for Julie's broken heart. They decided that one day they would remind her of her time as an angel child and restore to her a portion of her glorious black wings. Years passed, and Julie grew to be a stunning woman with long, chestnut ringlets of hair. But she felt shame and embarrassment because of the dark hair that grew on her back. The gods decided it was time to remind Julie of her wings. One day, as she stared in the mirror at herself with disdain, she noticed that the hair on her back was the imprint of beautiful black wings.

Julie's story forever changed the way she saw her body. The hair was no longer a source of shame but a whimsical tale of beauty and grace. What body shame taught her to hate she taught herself to love through the magic of a new story. We have the power to change the narrative of body shame in our lives. We are not bound to the tales of teasing and criticism we were subjected to as children. The good news is we are the authors of our own lives. Let's make every day an ode to radical self-love.

### Unapologetic Inquiry #30

*As children, we loved the unconstrained power of imagination we encountered in fairy tales. We could be an opulent princess, a cunning wizard, a talking dog. There were no boundaries around our possibility. Making a new story reconnects us with our unbounded possibility. What story have you been telling yourself that is binding your possibility? What would be possible if that story were different?*

## Pillar 4: Collective Compassion

### Tool 9: Be in a Community

In her book *The Gifts of Imperfection*, Brené Brown writes, "One of the greatest barriers to connection is the cultural importance we place on 'going it alone.' "[12] Somehow, we've come to equate success with not needing anyone. Many of us are willing to extend a helping hand, but we're very reluctant to reach out for help when we need it ourselves. It's as if we've divided the world into "those who offer help" and "those who need help." The truth is that we are both. Radical self-love is not a solo journey. A complicated and multilayered amalgamation of systems, structures, and experiences authored our body shame and built the larger social complex of body terrorism. We cannot dismantle that system in isolation. Science has much to offer us in our efforts to subvert the internal and external forces of body shame.

In the study of infectious diseases, epidemiologists use what is called the "epidemiological triad" to explain how pathogens spread from person to person.[13] This triad consists of an agent, a host, and an environment. *Agent* refers to the specific pathogen present in the triad. *Host* denotes whatever vessel (or conditions within a vessel) allows the agent to thrive. The *environment* consists of the external forces that foster the transmission of the agent to the host. When any of these three elements is disrupted, the trajectory of the disease is halted. In the work of radical self-love, body shame is the dis-ease, we are the hosts, and body terrorism is the environment.

Body shame thrives because our world cultivates and nurtures body terrorism through media, government, and culture. Society then transmits the pathogen of body shame to susceptible hosts (us), who carry it around and pass it on due to the internal conditions of stigma and shame. Being in community is how we interrupt the triad. Our refusal to host body shame in secrecy and isolation is the death knell of this dis-ease. Our perception of vulnerability as weakness is a function of body terrorism. Any belief that keeps us disconnected from our truth and from others will always be antithetical to radical self-love. Vulnerability gives us access to our wonder and magic through the eyes of others. Through this, we get the opportunity to see ourselves anew. To move beyond the narrative of individuality is to move beyond the narrative of scarcity and not-enoughness. It is in community that our stories are held up to the light of connection and we begin to see clearly how we are having a shared experience of being human with other humans—stories, fear, fog, and all.

It is critical that we find communities of care and compassion. In their absence, we are relegated to an echo chamber of pathological body hatred and oppression. Radical self-love environments are all around us, and thanks to the power of technology we can find people all over the world who are committed to interrupting body shame. Hint: www.TheBodyIsNotAnApology.com is a fabulous place to start!

### Unapologetic Inquiry #31

*What have you been holding in secrecy, shame, or embarrassment? How has it kept you disconnected from others? What are you willing to let go of for the sake of connection?*

**Tool 10: Give Yourself Some Grace**

This book, just like life, makes you no promises, but I would like to offer you one guarantee. I assure you that after you have read this entire book from cover to cover, you will still have days when you do not love your body. Here's the good news: it is perfectly okay! Let's just say you skipped all thirty thousand words of writing up to this point and through some happenstance of page sorcery landed on this page. I would personally congratulate you for arriving at the Holy Grail of the ten tools: grace. Even if you categorically rejected every piece of information you have been given thus far, tool 10 will still guide you to the unapologetic power of radical self-love. As long as we live in a world constructed of body shame and body terrorism, the radical self-love journey will be a daunting one at times. Despite my having all the pillars, tools, and unapologetic inquiries at my disposal, and running an entire organization focused exclusively on radical self-love, there are still days when I do not like this black, queer, fat, neurodivergent body.

Does this mean I am a radical self-love failure? No, it means I am a human being living in a world that still profits from body shame. Every day we awake to messages that reinforce the narrative that we are deficient. The body-shame amplifier will occasionally ring loud enough to feel like it is drowning out the chorus of our divinity. On those days, the work is still to love. Religious people consider grace the free and unmerited favor of God. Free and unmerited favor is a gift we can extend to ourselves regardless of faith or doctrine. We do not have to earn radical self-love. Our perfect execution of each pillar and tool will not get us a higher grade in the radical self-love class. The act of giving yourself some grace is the practice of loving the you that does not like your body. On the days we feel the most deficient, the most chased down by the dog of shame, what is being called forth from us is more love—not because we earned it but because we never had to. To give grace to oneself is to move beyond words like *worthy* and *deserving*, terms that still imply qualification and quantity. When we recognize ourselves as the embodiment of radical self-love, we stop trying to assess our worth. We begin to understand that it is inherent and unquantifiable. Love just is. We just are . . . love.

> **Radical Reflection**
> *The most powerful antidote to a world of body terrorism is a world of compassion. Giving yourself the gift of grace is an act of revolution!*

# Conclusion

Last summer, I sat on a hotel rooftop in Bahia, Brazil, with a gaggle of raucous and revolutionary Black feminist change makers. Over the course of three days these women, who were flung there from every corner of the world, detonated my mind with their interminable brilliance and insight. They were unquestionably some of the most bad-ass humans I had ever met. Sipping caipirinhas and cackling into the blue-black sky, my favorite rabble-rouser of the group, longtime activist and artist Kai (pronounced Kai-ee), in her half-teasing, wholly provocative way, queried the group, "We doing all this fighting for liberation. Any of y'all know what liberation looks like?"

Kai slapped the question down on the table like a dead fish, and the whole group was dumbstruck for a second. Quickly, answers began to stammer out of mouths like closing-time drunkards. It appeared many of us had never really given ourselves permission to ponder what a world rid of oppression might look like. My friends and comrades who were deeply involved in political movements from Ecuador to Houston, from farmworkers' rights to the Movement for Black Lives, wrestled with that small knot of a question well into the early morning hours. For many of us, the fight was so incessant, insisting on our every mental and emotional fiber for our survival, that rarely had we been given a moment to think about what might exist in our lives or on the planet when we finished fighting.

My answer was swift but silent. I said only to myself, "Radical self-love." Torn by what felt at once profoundly true and absurdly small, insignificant up against the global powers of oppression, I kept my answer inside. How could a concept so simple occupy the spaces that marginalization and separation had seemed to fill for centuries? But I knew that my follow-up question was a lie. My doubts were not about the efficacy of radical self-love. My doubts were about me. How dare I believe I have any answers for such complicated geopolitical and social quandaries? Who am I to even speak to these issues? How quickly the voice of self-doubt and deficiency ran in to fill the space in my head where radical self-love should have resided. My fear was not about what I didn't know. Example after example has apprised me of the same truth: the only thing that kills the slow, poisonous choke of body shame and body terrorism that dwells in each of us is radical self-love. That truth is not of me but through me, just like the first time I uttered the words "The body is not an apology." My work is simply to be a willing vessel for its message.

If I could go back to that night on a rooftop in Brazil and answer Kai's question, I would say, loudly and unapologetically, "Liberation is the opportunity for every human, no matter their body, to have unobstructed access to their highest self; for every human to live in radical self-love." I did not say it that night, but I am saying it now, to you, and I am not the least bit sorry.

# Notes

## Prologue

1. B. Brown, *Daring Greatly: How the Courage to Be Vulnerable Transforms the Way We Live, Love, Parent, and Lead* (London, UK: Penguin, 2012), 69.

2. M. Williamson, "The Spiritual Purpose of Relationships" (lecture, Los Angeles, CA, January 3, 2016).

## Chapter 1

1. S. L. Cano, "Angela Davis to Speak March 4 at New York City Unity Rally," *Peoples World,* February 28, 2017, http://www.peoplesworld.org/article/angela -davis-to-speak-march-4-at-new-york-city-unity-rally.

2. L. S. Cahill and M. A. Farley, *Embodiment, Morality, and Medicine* (The Netherlands: AA Dordrecht, Kluwer Academic Publishers, 1995).

3. M. Moseley, "Ten Things to Know About the Heartbreaking Story of Kalief Browder," *Essence,* March 2, 2017, http://www.essence.com/news/facts-about -kalief-browder-rikers-prison-documentary-JayZ.

4. C. Eisenstein, *The More Beautiful World Our Hearts Know Is Possible* (Berkeley, CA: North Atlantic Books, 2013).

5. Maureen Benson is a general rock star and founder and CEO of the organization Education Is a Vital Sign.

6. Definition of *radical,* Dictionary.com, accessed February 28, 2017, http://www .dictionary.com/browse/radical.

7. N. Ghandnoosh, "Race and Punishment: Racial Perceptions of Crime and Support for Punitive Policies," The Sentencing Project, October 3, 2014, http:// sentencingproject.org/wp-content/uploads/2015/11/Race-and-Punishment.pdf.

8. C. Liebowitz, "Explaining Inspiration Porn to Non-Disabled People," The Body Is Not an Apology, September 24, 2015, https://thebodyisnotanapology.com /magazine/explaining-inspiration-porn-to-non-disabled-people/.

9. "Africans in America," PBS, January 12, 2017, http://www.pbs.org/wgbh/aia /part2/2narr5.html.

10. "Voting Rights Act Timeline," ACLU, March 4, 2005, https://www.aclu.org /files/assets/voting_rights_act_timeline20111222.pdf.

11. Amend the Code for Marriage Equality Act of 2015, H.R. 2976, 114th Congress (2015–2016), July 8, 2015, https://www.congress.gov/bill /114th-congress/house-bill/2976.

12. P. Karp, "Marriage Equality Plebiscite Bill Voted Down in Senate," *The Guardian,* November 7, 2016, https://www.theguardian.com/australia-news /2016/nov/07/marriage-equality-plebiscite-bill-set-to-fail-as-nxt-vows-to-block -it-in-senate.

13. C. Domonoske and J. Doubek, "North Carolina Repeals Portions of Controversial 'Bathroom Bill,' " NPR, March 30, 2017, http://www.npr.org/sections/thetwo -way/2017/03/30/522009335/north-carolina-lawmakers-governor-announce -compromise-to-repeal-bathroom-bill.

14. "Persons with a Disability: Labor Force Characteristics," Bureau of Labor Statistics, June 21, 2016, https://www.bls.gov/news.release/disabl.htm.

15. K. Crenshaw, "Mapping the Margins: Intersectionality, Identity Politics, and Violence Against Women of Color," *Stanford Law Review* 43, no. 6 (1991): 1241, doi:10.2307/1229039.

16. H. Blank, "Real Women," blog post by Hanne Blank, May 5, 2017, http://www .hanneblank.com/blog/real-women/.

17. J. Gallagher, " 'Memories' Pass Between Generations," BBC, December 1, 2013, http://www.bbc.com/news/health-25156510.

18. "The Death of Emmett Till," History.com, accessed Nov, 23, 2016, http://www .history.com/this-day-in-history/the-death-of-emmett-till.

19. J. Sauers, "French *Elle's* First 'Curvy' Issue Introduces Us to Tara Lynn Capes," *Jezebel,* March 30, 2010, https://jezebel.com/5505614/french-elles-first-curvy -issue-introduces-us-to-tara-lynn-capes/.

20. S. Taylor, "Mission, Vision, and History," The Body Is Not an Apology, accessed Jan 30, 2017, https://thebodyisnotanapology.com/about-tbinaa/history -mission-and-vision/.

21. "Acceptance vs. Resignation," Secular Buddhism, February 24, 2016, https://secularbuddhism.com/acceptance-vs-resignation/.

22. T. R. Echeverria, "Audre Lorde: A Black, Lesbian, Mother, Socialist, Warrior, Poet," Solidarity, February 18, 2012, https://www.solidarity-us.org/site/node/3525.

23. Health at Every Size supports people of all sizes in addressing their health directly by encouraging the adoption of healthy behaviors. It is an inclusive

movement, recognizing that our social characteristics, such as our size, race, national origin, sexuality, gender, disability status, and other attributes, are assets. It acknowledges and challenges the structural and systemic forces that impinge on living well. See https://haescommunity.com/.

24. D. Burgard, "The Danger of Poodle Science," YouTube video, February 23, 2015, https://www.youtube.com/watch?v=H89QQfXtc-k.

25. "You are in the right place" is a common greeting for newcomers to twelve-step meetings. See https://en.wikipedia.org/wiki/Twelve-step_program (accessed January 15, 2017).

## Chapter 2

1. R. Bender, "The Age Girls Become Self-Conscious About Their Bodies," *Yahoo! News*, January 12, 2016, https://www.yahoo.com/news/the-age-girls-become-self -1338923817869366.html.

2. "Webinars and Online Courses," The Body Is Not an Apology, accessed January 30, 2017, https://thebodyisnotanapology.com/radical-education /webinars/.

3. For preferred terminology refer to the website Gender Diversity. Accessed November 23, 2016, http://www.genderdiversity.org/resources/terminology /#gendervariance.

4. A. H. Grossman and A. R. D'augell, "Transgender Youth and Life-Threatening Behaviors," *Suicide and Life-Threatening Behavior* 37, no. 5 (2007): 527–37, http://onlinelibrary.wiley.com/doi/10.1521/suli.2007.37.5.527 /abstract.

5. M. B. Brewer, "In-Group Bias in the Minimal Intergroup Situation: A Cognitive-Motivational Analysis," *Psychological Bulletin* 86, no. 2 (1979): 307–24, http://psycnet.apa.org/psycinfo/1979-25967-001.

6. "DBR MTV Bias Survey Summary," April 2014, p. 3, https://www.evernote .com/shard/s4/sh/5edc56c3-f8c8-483f-a459-2c47192d0bb8/a0ba0ce883749f4e 613d6a6338bb4455/res/5cff2161-7c98-4c9a-9830-a900c7496644/DBR_MTV _Bias_Survey_Executive_Summary.pdf.

7. "Get the Facts," About-Face.org, November 15, 2012, https://www.about-face .org/educate-yourself/get-the-facts/.

8. S. Sumapong, "Toxic Masculinity and the Negative Effects on Men," Good Men Project, November 18, 2016, https://goodmenproject.com/featured-content /toxic-masculinity-and-the-negative-effects-on-men-babb/.

9. C. Knorr, "Boys and Body Image," Common Sense Media, January 5, 2015, https://www.commonsensemedia.org/blog/boys-and-body-image#.

10. J. Bakutyte, "A Look at the History of Women's Beauty," *A Plus*, November 5, 2014, http://aplus.com/a/history-female-beauty-standards?no_monetization=true.

11. K. Gaylor, "A Royal Queer: Hatshepsut and Gender Construction in Ancient Egypt," *Shift Journal* 8 (2015): 1–11, http://shiftjournal.org/wp-content/uploads/2015/11/4_Gaylord.pdf.

12. "Timeline: Transgender Through History," *Doc Zone*, CBC/Radio Canada, April 10, 2013, http://www.cbc.ca/doczone/features/timeline-transgender-through-history.

13. D. R. Roediger, *Working Toward Whiteness: How America's Immigrants Became White: The Strange Journey from Ellis Island to the Suburbs* (New York: Basic Books, 2010).

14. "Ad Age Advertising Century: Timeline," *Ad Age*, March 29, 1999, http://adage.com/article/special-report-the-advertising-century/ad-age-advertising-century-timeline/143661/.

15. "Worldwide Ad Spending Growth Revised Downward," EMarketer, April 21, 2016, https://www.emarketer.com/Article/Worldwide-Ad-Spending-Growth-Revised-Downward/1013858.

16. "Global Cosmetics Market 2015–2020: Market Was $460 Billion in 2014 and Is Estimated to Reach $675 Billion by 2020," *Business Wire*, July 27, 2015, http://www.businesswire.com/news/home/20150727005524/en/Research-Markets-Global-Cosmetics-Market-2015-2020-Market.

17. "List of Countries by Projected GDP," www.StatisticsTimes.com, International Monetary Fund World Economic Outlook (October 2016), October 21, 2016, http://statisticstimes.com/economy/countries-by-projected-gdp.php.

18. "Self-Image and Media Influence," Just Say Yes, February 28, 2017, https://www.justsayyes.org/topics/self-image-media-influences/.

19. M. Mychaskiw, "Report: Women Spend an Average of $15,000 on Makeup in Their Lifetimes," InStyle.com, May 21, 2015, http://www.instyle.com/beauty/15-under-15-best-bargain-beauty-products.

20. "Hot, in style, popular, 'damn, that song was poppin' back in the day,' " definition of *poppin'*, Urban Dictionary, accessed May 17, 2017, https://www.urbandictionary.com/define.php?term=poppin.

21. G. Beemyn, "Transgender Terminology," Cornell.edu, April 27, 2017, https://hr.cornell.edu/sites/default/files/trans%20terms.pdf.

22. "Laws Against the LGBT," Galloway Family Foundation, accessed January 30, 2017, http://www.gallowayfoundation.org/category-anti-lgbt-laws/.

23. "Health Requirements," New Zealand Immigration Concepts, accessed January 30, 2017, https://www.new-zealand-immigration.com/.

24. S. Chemaly, "Ten Ridiculously Sexist and Dangerous Laws from Around the World," *Huffington Post,* February 15, 2015, http://www.huffingtonpost.com /soraya-chemaly/10-ridiculously-sexist-laws-around-the-world_b_6679970 .html.

25. H. Schwarz, "Following Reports of Forced Sterilization of Female Prison Inmates, California Passes Ban," *The Washington Post,* September 26, 2014, https://www.washingtonpost.com/blogs/govbeat/wp/2014/09/26/following -reports-of-forced-sterilization-of-female-prison-inmates-california-passes-ban /?utm_term=.367b41a1fc43.

26. A. N. Ltd, "With This Ring, I Thee Abduct," *Times of Malta,* February 25, 2015, http://www.timesofmalta.com/articles/view/20150225/local/with-this-ring-i -thee-abduct.557594.

27. D. Artavia, "Greece Reinstates Forced HIV Testing," *Plus,* July 22, 2013, http://www.hivplusmag.com/case-studies/world-news/2013/07/22/greece -reinstates-forced-hiv-testing.

28. "History of Women Governors," Center for American Women in Politics, accessed January 30, 2017, http://www.cawp.rutgers.edu/history-women -governors.

29. "Fast Facts About American Governors," website of Rutgers University, February 27, 2017, http://governors.rutgers.edu/on-governors/us-governors /fast-facts-about-american-governors/.

30. "Female World Leaders Currently in Power," World Bank, accessed January 30, 2017, http://data.worldbank.org/indicator/SG.GEN.PARL.ZS.

31. N. Wolfe, *The Beauty Myth: How Images of Beauty Are Used Against Women* (New York: HarperPerennial, 2002), 187.

32. "List of Minority Governors and Lieutenant Governors in the United States," www.ebooklibrary.org, January 30, 2017, http://ebooklibrary.org/Articles /List%20of%20minority%20governors%t.

33. I. Langtree, "List of Physically Disabled World Leaders and Politicians," Disabled-World.com, July 29, 2015, https://www.disabled-world.com/disability /awareness/leaders-pollies.php#u.

34. C. Domonoske, "For First Time, Openly LGBT Governor Elected: Oregon's Kate Brown," NPR, November 9, 2016, http://www.npr.org/sections/thetwo-way /2016/11/09/501338927/for-first-time-openly-lgbt-governor-elected-oregons -kate-brown.

35. S. Tavernise, "U.S. Suicide Rate Surges to a 30-Year High," *NY Times,* April 22, 2016, https://www.nytimes.com/2016/04/22/health/us-suicide-rate-surges-to-a -30-year-high.html?_r=0.

36. R. Gabrielson, R. Grochowski Jones, E. Sagara, "Deadly Force, in Black and White," ProPublica, December 24, 2014, https://www.propublica.org/article/deadly-force-in-black-and-white.

37. "More Than 115 Anti-LGBTQ Bills Introduced in 30 States," Human Rights Campaign, accessed Janueary 10, 2017, https://www.hrc.org/blog/more-than-115-anti-lgbtq-bills-introduced-in-30-states.

38. F. Fox, "Leelah Alcorn's Suicide: Conversion Therapy Is Child Abuse," *Time,* January 8, 2015, http://time.com/3655718/leelah-alcorn-suicide-transgender-therapy.

39. Definition of *terrorism,* Merriam-Webster.com, accessed January 29, 2017, https://www.merriam-webster.com/dictionary/terrorism.

40. "What Is Body Terrorism?," The Body Is Not an Apology, accessed January 29, 2017, https://thebodyisnotanapology.com/about-tbinaa/what-is-body-terrorism/.

## Chapter 3

1. From the website of Davide Carrera, accessed April 23, 2017, http://www.davidecarrera.com/.

2. "Arabs as Terrorists: The Power of Media Images," Society of Personality and Social Psychology, December 9, 2012, https://spsptalks.wordpress.com/2012/12/07/arabs-as-terrorists-the-power-of-media-images.

3. A. Willingham, "Chances of a Refugee Killing You—and Other Surprising Immigration Stats," CNN.com, accessed January 30, 2017, http://www.cnn.com/2017/01/30/politics/immigration-stats-by-the-numbers-trnd/.

4. J. E. Short, "How Much Media?," Business.tivo.com, accessed January 30, 2017, https://business.tivo.com/content/dam/tivo/resources/tivo-HMM-Consumer-Report-2013_Release.pdf.

5. E. Ensler, "Suddenly My Body," TED video, December 2011 https://www.ted.com/talks/eve_ensler.

6. N. Waheed, "Three," www.wordsfortheyear.com, June 1, 2015, https://wordsfortheyear.com/2015/06/04/three-by-nayyirah-waheed/.

7. A. C. Liebowitz, "Here's What Neurodiversity Is—And What It Means for Feminism," Everyday Feminism, March 3, 2016, http://everydayfeminism.com/2016/03/neurodiversity-101/.

## Chapter 4

1. "Understanding Implicit Bias," Kirwan Institute for the Study of Race and Ethnicity, accessed January 30, 2017, http://kirwaninstitute.osu.edu/research/understanding-implicit-bias/.

2. L. Watson, Lilla: Internation Women's Network, January 27, 2010, https://lillanetwork.wordpress.com/about/.

3. G. L. Boggs, *Living for Change: An Autobiography* (Minneapolis: University of Minnesota Press, 2016), 146.

4. *Slavery by Another Name* (documentary), directed by Samuel D. Pollard, aired February 13, 2012, accessed January 30, 2012, http://www.pbs.org/tpt/slavery-by-another-name/themes/convict-leasing/.

5. "Black Codes," History.com, 2010, http://www.history.com/topics/black-history/black-codes.

6. M. Alexander, *The New Jim Crow* (New York: New Press, 2012), 2.

7. M. Kennedy, "Trump's Immigration Order Is 'Not a Ban on Muslims,' Homeland Security Chief Says," January 31, 2017, http://www.npr.org/sections/thetwo-way/2017/01/31/512678699/trumps-immigration-order-is-not-a-ban-on-muslims-homeland-security-chief-says.

8. "Six Other Times the US Has Banned Immigrants," AlJazeera.com, January 29, 2017, http://www.aljazeera.com/indepth/features/2017/01/times-banned-immigrants-170128183528941.html.

9. "Immigration," HIV Law and Policy, accessed Janueary 30, 2017, https://www.hivlawandpolicy.org/issues/immigration.

10. D. Merica, "Hillary Clinton Speaks with Black Lives Matter Activists," CNN.com, August 18, 2015, http://www.cnn.com/2015/08/18/politics/hillary-clinton-black-lives-matter-meeting/.

11. "Hillary Clinton: Equality Is About Changing Hearts and Minds," YouTube video, October 21, 2016, https://www.youtube.com/watch?v=kuxdbBPSnas.

12. A. Gomez and D. Agren, "First Protected DREAMer Is Deported Under Trump," *USA Today,* April 18, 2017, https://www.usatoday.com/story/news/world/2017/04/18/first-protected-dreamer-deported-under-trump/100583274/.

13. M. Inman, "You're not going to believe what I am about to tell you," The Oatmeal.com. July 23, 2017, http://theoatmeal.com/comics/believe.

14. J. L. Anderson, *Che Guevara: A Revolutionary Life* (New York: Grove Press, 2010), 178.

15. A.A., S. (n.d.). Promises—Alcoholic Anonymous. Retrieved from https://step12.com/promises.html.

## Chapter 5

1. Jill Scott interview, *Dave Chappelle's Block Party,* YouTube video, 1:00, posted June 29, 2009, https://www.youtube.com/watch?v=Cr-lRfbxzYA.

2. J. Baker, *Things No One Will Tell Fat Girls* (Berkeley, CA: Seal Press, 2015), 3.

3. Kai Cheng Thom, "Not Born This Way: On Transitioning as a Transwoman Who Has Never Felt 'Trapped in the Wrong Body,'" *XOJane*, July 9, 2015, http://www.xojane.com/issues/im-a-transwoman-who-never-felt-trapped-in-the -wrong-body.

4. J. David Creswell, et al., "Alterations in Resting-State Functional Connectivity Link Mindfulness Meditation with Reduced Interleukin-6: A Randomized Controlled Trial," *Biological Psychiatry* 80, no. 1 (2016): 53–61, http://repository .cmu.edu/cgi/viewcontent.cgi?article=2407&context=psychology.

5. "We Remember Bad Times Better than Good," ScienceDaily.com, August 28, 2007, https://www.sciencedaily.com/releases/2007/08/070828110711.htm.

6. M. Wei, MD JD, "How Mantras Calm Your Mind," *The Huffington Post*, August 14, 2015, http://www.huffingtonpost.com/marlynn-wei-md-jd/how -mantras-calm-your-mind_b_7989674.html.

7. "What Is Binary?," WhatIs.com, accessed November 26, 2016, http://whatis .techtarget.com/definition/binary.

8. Definition of *binary*, Free Sociology Dictionary, November 26, 2016, http:// sociologydictionary.org/gender-binary/.

9. M. Y. Roth, et al., "Self-Detection Remains a Key Method of Breast Cancer Detection for U.S. Women," *Journal of Women's Health* 20, no. 8 (2011): 1135–39, https://www.ncbi.nlm.nih.gov/pubmed/21675875.

10. M. Castleman, "The Most Important Sexual Statistic," *Psychology Today*, March 16, 2009, https://www.psychologytoday.com/blog/all-about-sex/200903 /the-most-important-sexual-statistic.

11. CompilarizTVi, "'Babies Is a Better Dancers than You' Compilation," YouTube video, posted April 1, 2013, https://www.cdc.gov/bam/teachers/documents/epi _1_triangle.pdf.

12. B. Brown, *The Gifts of Imperfection: Let Go of Who You Think You're Supposed to Be and Embrace Who You Are* (Center City, MN: Hazelden, 2010), 68.

13. "Agent, Host, Environment," www.cdc.gov, accessed January 30, 2017, https://www.cdc.gov/bam/teachers/documents/epi_1_triangle.pdf.

# Radical Resources

The only way to fight an entire world built on body shame is to build a world of radical self-love around ourselves. Leaving the land of body shame can feel like the world's loneliest exile, but it need not be. There are thousands of activists, organizations, and media sources doing work to create a just world for our different bodies. Below I've listed only a few. Visit these websites to learn more.

## Radical Self-Love

The Body Is Not an Apology    www.thebodyisnotanapology.com/

## Intersectional Feminism Media

Everyday Feminism    www.everydayfeminism.com/

The Establishment    https://theestablishment.co/

Guerilla Feminism    www.guerrillafeminism.org/

Wear Your Voice    http://wearyourvoicemag.com/

Ravishly    www.ravishly.com/

About Face    www.about-face.org/

## Weight Stigma Resources

Association for Size Diversity and Health (ASDAH)
        https://www.sizediversityandhealth.org/

National Association to Advance Fat Acceptance (NAAFA)
        https://www.naafaonline.com/dev2/

NOLOSE    http://nolose.org/

Binge Eating and Disorders Association    http://bedaonline.com/

Health at Every Size    https://haescommunity.com/

## Racial Justice Resources

The Movement for Black Lives    https://policy.m4bl.org/
Race Forward    www.raceforward.org/
Black Youth Project 100    http://byp100.org/
Showing Up for Racial Justice    www.showingupforracialjustice.org/
United We Dream    https://unitedwedream.org/

## Disability Justice Resources

Disability Justice    http://disabilityjustice.org/
Sins Invalid    http://www.sinsinvalid.org/
Leah Lakshmi Piepzna-Samarasinha
    http://www.brownstargirl.org/
ADAPT    http://adapt.org/
Icarus Project    http://theicarusproject.net/

## LGBTQIAA Resources

Transgender Law Center (TLC)    https://transgenderlawcenter.org/
GLAAD    www.glaad.org/
Southerners on New Ground    http://southernersonnewground.org/
Astrea Foundation    www.astraeafoundation.org/
Trans Lifeline    www.translifeline.org/   US: (877) 565-8860
                                                    Canada: (877) 330-6366

## Aging Resources

National Council on Aging    www.ncoa.org/
Services and Advocacy for GLBT Elders    www.sageusa.org/
National Asian Pacific Center on Aging    http://napca.org/
HelpAge USA    www.helpageusa.org/

# Acknowledgments

When I connect to how deeply I am loved, I weep and a new layer of shame melts away. This book would have been an impossibility if not for the epic love of an entire planet of humans on every continent. For every phone call, text, or video message reminding me to keep going, thank you. I love you. For every "Sonya, I brought you a horchata latte (or flowers) or mailed you a letter (or sent artwork or a care package) because you said you were lonely (thirsty, sad, scared, exhausted, confused) yesterday on Facebook." *Thank you* for loving me like this. Your love saves me daily. Thanks to my dad, Daryl Taylor, for handling with such grace the fact that his daughter is naked all over the internet and on the cover of this book. Love you! Thanks to my siblings, Daryl, Jeanne, and Jozlynn. Through each of you I have learned to love the Taylor forehead and our tender connection. Can I just say, I have the *best* grandma on the planet? Thank you, Kathryn Taylor, for being the embodiment of nurture and care. Thanks to my aunts, uncles, cousins—there are so many of y'all. I love each of you. You are my connection to home.

I once had a date tell me that you could only have one best friend because the word *best* implies only one. He desperately needed tool 5: banish the binary. I have so many best friends, folks I love like we share DNA sequencing. I am blessed that they let me share in their lives. Thank you Aleshia, Jaimie, and Monique for being "ride or die" for more than a quarter century! You've seen the full arc of this journey and have stuck around. I love you. Let's keep making memories.

Thank you Charneice, Gayle, and Chris. We met through the magic of words, but we chose to become family. Our futures are epic! Let's keep going. Maureen and Denise, to say none of this would have been possible without your insight, cheerleading, encouragement, protection, and willingness to do all the hardest radical self-love work with me would be a paltry summation. I am because we are. We will always be we to me. I love you.

Radical self-love has demanded I take radical care of this perfect but fragile mind of mine. This would have been an unthinkable task were it not for Dr. Jacelyn Bronte. I am certain I make people jealous because I go on so about my rock-star therapist. Her guidance and unconditional love over the years have given me the safety I have needed to explore the difference between fear and danger. It has allowed me to heal places I feared would forever be broken. Thank you. Additionally, this book *literally* would not have been completed without the breakthrough Rapid Transformation Therapy practice of my friend Hilary Hayes. If you have a block, she has a clearing (and a horchata latte) for you. I love you.

To The Body Is Not an Apology Leadership Circle, you are possibility made flesh. Your insights and vulnerabilities capture the hearts of hundreds of thousands of people and change their lives. You have translated the vision of radical self-love into the global work of transformation. Your compassion for my imperfect leadership and your endless generosity of spirit sustain me. Whenever I want to quit I remember that you have not, and I keep going. I commit to never stop working to make TBINAA an organization in which your most powerful gifts can be manifest and your labor can be rewarded.

To the organizers and activists that fight every day for the most marginalized bodies, thank you. Your unsung work is our only access to liberation. Keep stoking the flames of freedom. I believe that we will win.

If you are reading this, thank you. I am because you are.

# Index

# About the Author

**Sonya Renee Taylor** is the founder and radical executive officer of The Body Is Not An Apology, a digital media and education company committed to radical self-love and body empowerment as the foundational tool for social justice and global transformation. TBINAA.com reaches over one million people in 140 countries each month with its articles and content focused on the intersection of bodies, personal transformation, and social justice. Sonya is also an international-award-winning performance poet, activist, speaker, and transformational leader whose work has global reach. She has appeared across the United States and in New Zealand, Australia, England, Scotland, Sweden, Germany, Brazil, Canada, and the Netherlands. Sonya and her work have been seen, heard, and read on HBO, BET, MTV, TV One, NPR, PBS, CNN, Oxygen Network, The New York Times, New York magazine, MSNBC.com, Today.com, Huffington Post, Vogue Australia, Shape .com, Ms. magazine, and many more forums. In 2016, she was invited by the Obama White House to speak on the intersection of LGBTQIAA and disability issues. She has shared stages with such luminaries as Angela Davis, Van Jones, Naomi Klein, Amy Goodman, Carrie Mae Weems, Theaster Gates, Harry Bela-

*fonte, Dr. Cornel West, Hillary Rodham Clinton, the late Amiri Baraka, and numerous others. Sonya lives in Oakland, California, with her Yorkshire terrier, Anastasia Duchess. She continues to perform, speak, and facilitate workshops globally. Visit her at www.sonya-renee.com.*

# About TBINAA

www.TBINAA.com

**The Body Is Not An Apology** *is a digital media and education company committed to cultivating global Radical Self Love and Body Empowerment as the foundational tool for social justice and global transformation. We believe that discrimination, social inequality, and injustice are manifestations of our inability to make peace with the body, our own and others'. Utilizing the power of technology, media, education, and community building, The Body Is Not An Apology fosters global, radical, unapologetic self-love, which translates to radical human love and action in service toward a more just, equitable, and compassionate world. Join the hundreds of thousands of people who are reading new radical self-love articles and content daily at www.TheBodyIsNotAnApology.com.*

# Berrett–Koehler
## BK Publishers

**Berrett-Koehler** is an independent publisher dedicated to an ambitious mission: *Connecting people and ideas to create a world that works for all.*

We believe that the solutions to the world's problems will come from all of us, working at all levels: in our organizations, in our society, and in our own lives. Our BK Business books help people make their organizations more humane, democratic, diverse, and effective (we don't think there's any contradiction there). Our BK Currents books offer pathways to creating a more just, equitable, and sustainable society. Our BK Life books help people create positive change in their lives and align their personal practices with their aspirations for a better world.

All of our books are designed to bring people seeking positive change together around the ideas that empower them to see and shape the world in a new way.

And we strive to practice what we preach. At the core of our approach is Stewardship, a deep sense of responsibility to administer the company for the benefit of all of our stakeholder groups including authors, customers, employees, investors, service providers, and the communities and environment around us. Everything we do is built around this and our other key values of quality, partnership, inclusion, and sustainability.

This is why we are both a B-Corporation and a California Benefit Corporation—a certification and a for-profit legal status that require us to adhere to the highest standards for corporate, social, and environmental performance.

We are grateful to our readers, authors, and other friends of the company who consider themselves to be part of the BK Community. We hope that you, too, will join us in our mission.

### A BK Life Book

BK Life books help people clarify and align their values, aspirations, and actions. Whether you want to manage your time more effectively or uncover your true purpose, these books are designed to instigate infectious positive change that starts with you. Make your mark!

To find out more, visit **www.bkconnection.com**.

# Berrett–Koehler
## Publishers

Connecting people and ideas
to create a world that works for all

Dear Reader,

Thank you for picking up this book and joining our worldwide community of Berrett-Koehler readers. We share ideas that bring positive change into people's lives, organizations, and society.

**To welcome you, we'd like to offer you a free e-book.** You can pick from among twelve of our bestselling books by entering the promotional code **BKP92E** here: http://www.bkconnection.com/welcome.

When you claim your free e-book, we'll also send you a copy of our e-newsletter, the *BK Communiqué*. Although you're free to unsubscribe, there are many benefits to sticking around. In every issue of our newsletter you'll find

- A free e-book
- Tips from famous authors
- Discounts on spotlight titles
- Hilarious insider publishing news
- A chance to win a prize for answering a riddle

Best of all, our readers tell us, "Your newsletter is the only one I actually read." So claim your gift today, and please stay in touch!

Sincerely,

Charlotte Ashlock
Steward of the BK Website

Questions? Comments? Contact me at bkcommunity@bkpub.com.

**MIX**
Paper from
responsible sources
FSC www.fsc.org **FSC® C002589**

Certified

**B**

Corporation
bcorporation.net